Information Security Best Practices

205 Basic Rules

Information Security
Best Practices
205 Basic Rules

by
George L. Stefanek, Ph.D

BUTTERWORTH
HEINEMANN

An Imprint of Elsevier
BOSTON OXFORD AUCKLAND JOHANNESBURG MELBOURNE NEW DELHI

Butterworth-Heinemann is an imprint of Elsevier.

Copyright © 2002, Elsevier.

 Recognizing the importance of preserving what has been written, Elsevier prints its books on acid-free paper whenever possible.

 Elsevier supports the efforts of American Forests and the Global ReLeaf program in its campaign for the betterment of trees, forests, and our environment.

Library of Congress Cataloging-in-Publication Data
ISBN-13: 978-1-878707-96-3
ISBN-10: 1-878707-96-5
British Library Cataloguing-in-Publication Data
A catalogue record for this book is available from the British Library.

The publisher offers special discounts on bulk orders of this book.
For information, please contact:

Manager of Special Sales
Elsevier
225 Wildwood Avenue
Woburn, MA 01801-2041
Tel: 781-904-2500
Fax: 781-904-2620

For information on all Butterworth-Heinemann publications available, contact our World Wide Web home page at: http://www.bh.com

10 9 8 7 6 5 4 3

Printed in the United States of America

Contents

Acknowledgments

I would like to thank the following two systems administrators, Mark Draughn and Richard Serafin, for their help in reviewing this manual.

— *G. Stefanek*

Preface

I wrote this manual as a source of practical rules or "best practices" that a novice or practicing system administrator can follow to implement information security (INFOSEC) within their organization. It has been my experience that there are many information security practices that I use over and over in most environments. Much literature is available on network and data security that describes security concepts but offers so many different solutions to information security problems that it typically overwhelms both the novice and the experienced network administrator. In this book, I present a simple set of rules that I consider to be important in maintaining good information security. It is compiled as a set of rules that make up "best practices" for securing a network, based on my opinion and experience in implementing network solutions and solving security problems over many years.

These best practices are intended to be a "recipe" for setting up network and information security, but are not the only methodology to solve a problem. Some books compare INFOSEC solutions, but rarely recommend any one solution, since each network configuration and security policy is different. These best practices are proposed as rules in this guide. I've tried to narrow down the choices to a set of scenarios that cover most of the environments that will be encountered. Special environments such as military multi-level security are not extensively covered. It is my hope that this manual will take the mystery out of configuring an information security solution and provide a framework which the novice as well as experienced network administrator can follow and adapt to their network and data environment. Complying with all these practices will take dedication and a lot of work. However, using even a subset of these best practices will increase the security of your systems and network.

Information Security Attacks and Vulnerabilities

To understand why you need to implement information security, I first present a list of the types of attacks that hackers may launch against your network. The information security best practices that are presented in the following sections are designed to prevent these forms of attack and decrease vulnerabilities.

> **NOTE:** IF YOU SUSPECT THAT YOUR NETWORK IS CURRENTLY UNDER ATTACK, TURN IMMEDIATELY TO SECTION 19, *EMERGENCY RULES AGAINST ATTACK*, FOR ACTIONS YOU CAN TAKE THAT CAN SAVE DOWNTIME AND PREVENT DESTRUCTION OF INFORMATION!

1.1 SPAMMING

Spamming consists of an identified or unidentified source sending bulk mail to your site. In the nonmalicious form it consists of sending bulk advertising mail to many accounts at your site consistently, even multiple times a day. In the malicious form (e.g., email bombing) it consists of an attacker sending bulk mail until your mail server runs out of disk space. This type of attack consumes part or all of the communications bandwidth to your site and attempts to deny service to your mail server by keeping it busy and filling up its disk space. When the disk space is full, then the mail server will be unable to receive any additional mail. A variant of this attack consists of the hacker sending a single mail message to a mail server that includes a large forwarding list of mail addresses. Some mail servers will make copies of the mail message and attempt to send it to the forwarded destination addresses even though no legitimate account exists for the originator of the message.

1.2 VIRUSES

Computer viruses are compact packages of software that require a host (i.e., the computer) in order to replicate and possibly cause damage. Viruses can attack any part of a computer's software such as its boot block, operating system, file allocation (FAT) tables, EXE files, COM files and application program macros. Boot block viruses replace the boot block with virus code and relocate it to another disk location where data may be overwritten at that location. EXE and COM file viruses insert or append the virus code into these files. Some viruses take steps to conceal the addition of the code by modifying the file structure or making sure the CRC (Cyclic Redundancy Check) does not change. Even though viruses that infect a system may not make operation of the system catastrophic, they need to be cleaned up, which takes time. Cleaning up a virus requires removing it from the computer, from floppies, and from other systems that exchanged data with the infected system.

1.3 DENIAL OF SERVICE ATTACKS

Denial of service attacks disable a computer system by eating system resources until the system or applications come to a halt. Flooding a system with junk mail or synchronization (SYN) packets (i.e., SYN flood attack) are examples of denial of service attacks (see Section 1.10, IP Spoofing).

1.4 PASSWORD GUESSING

Most hackers gain illegal entry into remote computer systems by guessing passwords. It is surprising that so many system accounts have weak passwords. Most hackers gain access by guessing people's passwords using common names or combinations of letters. Also, password generation programs are commonly used that create passwords, usually a dictionary word, to try to gain access. If access is denied, another password is generated and the process is repeated. These password generation programs first try common words such as names, planets, places, etc.

1.5 WORMS

Once inside a computer, a hacker can place a program called a *worm* that self-replicates. Worm programs keep growing larger until disk space or memory is filled. These programs seek out unused resources and then consume them.

1.6 BACKDOOR

Once a hacker breaks into a system, code can be inserted somewhere on the system to create a secret backdoor that allows unauthorized access. The hacker may deposit a program on the system that allows backdoor access at will. Alternatively, the hacker can create his own innocuous-looking account that provides access to the system.

1.7 SWEEPER

Hackers may use a program called a *sweeper* that sweeps (i.e., deletes) all data from the system.

1.8 SNIFFERS

Sniffers are programs that monitor network traffic (i.e., packets) and can gather useful information that can be used in an attack. Hackers use sniffers to capture the first few hundred bytes of telnet, ftp, and rlogin sessions in order to obtain clear text passwords and other useful packet information. Once a single computer is compromised and a sniffer is installed, then all the remaining machines on the network can be compromised.

1.9 PACKET FORGE SPOOFING

This is a form of attack that involves the subtle alteration of data in a packet. A sophisticated hacker may be able to alter the data effectively in order to do damage to the intended target. This usually results in the receipt of wrong information (i.e., misinformation) that was modified by the hacker. From the attacker's point of view it is better to give the recipient the wrong information rather than no information.

1.10 IP SPOOFING

A SYN flood attack is a form of internet protocol (IP) spoofing that exploits the three-way handshake in the TCP/IP protocol that initiates every IP connection. This form of attack allows a hacker to fake his identity by sending SYN packets with a spoofed source address to a destination host. The destination host sends a SYN-ACK packet to the unsuspecting host with the spoofed address. The destination host waits for an ACK until there is a time-out. The destination machine connection buffer fills with incomplete connections until it stops accepting new connections. In another variation of this type of attack, the hacker probes a computer's ports. When an active port is found, the hacker sends multiple SYN packets to discover the sequence numbers of returning ACK/SYN packets. Another SYN packet that impersonates a trusted computer is sent by the hacker followed by an ACK with the correct sequence number, thus establishing a connection to the computer. The computer will transmit information to the hacker since it believes the connection is to a trusted host[1].

1.11 TROJAN HORSES

Trojan horses are software codes that enter the computer system through the front door. This type of software is embedded in a program or utility that the user believes to be harmless, such as a text editor or useful utility program. These programs are obtained voluntarily by the user to help with some task or problem. When the program is used, it then performs some malicious function such as deleting or copying files to another computer.

---

[1] Meinel, C., *"How Hackers Break In…"*, *Scientific American, October 1998, pp. 98-105.*

Anatomy of an Attack

This section provides an example of how a hacker might discover information and gain access to a network[2]. An attack on your system can come from either inside or outside your organization. *Protecting your systems only from external attack may be a fatal flaw in your security policy.* Most attacks, however, do come from the outside by either experienced hackers or inexperienced, newly budding hackers and take place during the night when risk of detection is low. The tools that a hacker needs to try to break into your network and systems are available on the Internet. Describing this process should enlighten the reader to the clever methods that may be employed by a hacker to gain access to your systems and network. More detail can be found in [Meinel98] and [Abene97], listed in the bibliography at the end of the book.

1. The hacker picks a target organization.

2. The hacker attempts to discover the organization's internet connections by issuing *whois* queries to InterNIC (Internet Network Information Center) to find the organization's DNS (Domain Name Service) servers.

---

[2] Abene, Mark, Kovacich, G. L. and Lutz, S. "Intrusion Detection Provides a Pound of Prevention," *Network Computing Online: The Technology Solutions Center.* 1997.

3. A DNS zone transfer is requested from the organization's DNS servers. This is a probe into the organization that may not be blocked by the organization's firewall (if they have one at all).

4. The hacker tries to discover the IP addresses of the filtering router, which is the organization's internet gateway, by probing the site with a program that will trace the route packets will travel. The organization's internal router or firewall will be the last hope before packets issued by the probe get dropped.

5. IP addresses for bastion host machines (see section 5.3) outside the firewall attempt to be found.

6. The bastion host machine ports are scanned to determine which ports are active and what system services are running that may be exploited.

7. If access can be gained into the machine, then the accounts database or password file is searched for existing usernames.

8. Password cracking programs are used to try to break into the administrator or "super-user" account. If access is gained, then that machine is entirely compromised and the hacker has free rein.

9. Next, to compromise other machines on the network, a password decryption program is run to get other username passwords. Some of the same passwords that are on bastion hosts may be used on machines inside the firewall. Also addresses and names of the internal machines may be discovered by checking the "hosts" file or other equivalent files residing on the bastion hosts.

10. Armed with this information, access to the internal machines is attempted via the compromised bastion host machine. Misconfigured or poorly configured firewalls are common. These may contain holes that allow access to internal networks to clever hackers. If entry is achieved by remote login to any of the internal machines, then a sniffer program can be run from the internal machine to discover clear-text password information flowing on the network and thereby enable hacked access into all the internal machines.

11. Once inside, then other access points within the internal network such as other firewalls or machines with modems are secured in case the original intrusion point is discovered. Phone numbers to modems may be published internally or in an administrator's directory. Else, a dialer program that scans the phone lines looking for modem carriers can be run. Internal PCs with modems are a perfect backdoor.

12. The attack progresses to compromise as many machines as possible with the ultimate goal to reach an organization's most mission-critical machines and those with sensitive information.

Awareness and Management Commitment to Security

The first step in implementing information security is to create a security policy. Before creating a security policy, however, an organization's management must consider arguments for the security risks: how security breaches may impact business, such as the reputation of the company if it is hacked (negative publicity), and the potential financial risk that is at stake. Also, some businesses, such as healthcare, will need to implement information security because it is required by law. If the risks to the organization are not perceived as high, or are not believable, then you will not be able to effectively enforce or maintain your security policy.

Much of the time management is simply not aware of the risks or does not fully understand them. They may not believe the organization is vulnerable to attack for some reason. Managers of small companies, for example, tend to downplay security risks. I have found a general lack of management awareness of security risks at all levels and types of organizations. Security at best is perceived as a necessary evil and at worst is seen as a costly and undesirable intrusion. It *must* be seen as an integral part of an organization's overall business strategy. Security risks must be translated in the minds of managers to financial loss, either through lost business, reduced productivity, lost data, revealed corporate secrets or compromised integrity. The threat by hackers *must* be perceived as real. Examples of recent hacker attacks on similar organizations may need to be presented to management, to get their attention.

If management does not agree to establish and enforce a security policy, then your enhancements to security may not stop your high-risk threats. The high-risk threats and the cost of mitigating these threats must be presented accurately and fully. Only then can management make a good decision. Since management may need to be educated as to the reality of the threat and its impact on the organization, the most potent argument is to clearly define the financial risks. It may be necessary to hire a third party to do the vulnerability analysis, as this often has a stronger impact with management.

Security Policy

Establishing a security policy is the starting point in designing a secure computer network. It is essential that a set of minimum security requirements be gathered, formalized and included as the basis of your security policy. This security policy must be enforceable by your organization and will create an additional cost to running and monitoring your network. This additional cost/benefit of a security policy must be understood and embraced by your organization's management in order to enhance and maintain network and system security.

The lack of an accepted and well-thought-out security policy and guidelines document is one of the major security vulnerabilities in most companies today. This section discusses several Best Practices related to the production of such a document. In addition, a generic security policy is provided in Appendix B and also on the accompanying CD-ROM. The importance of a meaningful security policy cannot be overemphasized.

INFOSEC Best Practice #1

Perform a threat analysis and risk analysis for your organization to determine the level of security that must be implemented.

First, identify all the threats to your computers and network; second, determine threat categories; third, perform the risk assessment; and, fourth, recommend action. Risk assessment should be performed by constructing a "consequence" matrix vs. "likelihood" matrix[3] as shown in Figure 4-1.

For each threat, construct a likelihood/consequence table. The "likelihood" rating for a threat can use categories such as A = remote, B = unlikely, C = likely, D = highly likely, and E = near certainty. The "Consequence" rating of the threat should use a point system where block 1 in the table = 0-1 points, block 2 = 2-3 points, block 3 = 4-6 points, block 4 = 7-9 points, block 5 = 9-11 points. Points are assigned

Figure 4-1:
Risk Rating Matrix

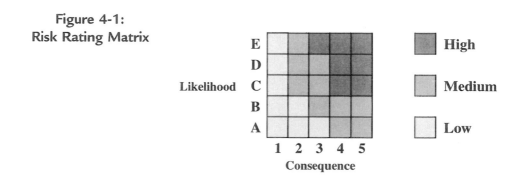

---

[3] NDIA, Undersea Warfare Systems Division, "INFOSEC Considerations for Submarine Systems Study, Technical Report II: Threat/Risk Decomposition", 1998.

based upon your subjective assessment of a compromise in security as an impact on functioning of your organization and data compromise. For instance, 5 points = organization grinds to a halt, loss of mission-critical systems; 3 points = some application(s) don't function, loss of non-mission-critical systems, but the organization can function; and 0 points = no loss of function. Data compromise points may be assigned as, for example, 2 points = compromise of sensitive data to people outside the organization; 1 point = compromise of sensitive data to people internal to the organization that should not have access; and 0 point = no compromise of data. This type of matrix will immediately highlight where to emphasize security. Also, a form should be created and filled out that: 1) identifies the threat, 2) gives solutions to the threat, 3) shows the likelihood of the threat (i.e., A, B, etc.), 4) gives the impact of the threat on an organization's function and data, and 5) shows the consequences of a compromise.

✓ INFOSEC Best Practice #2

Define a security policy for the entire site and use it as a guide for the network security architecture.

Define a policy that includes sections for confidentiality, integrity, availability, accountability, assurance, and enforcement, as described in the following paragraphs. The policy should address as much as possible of what is included in these sections according to risk and affordability. The general security policy described in this section was developed from DoD 5200.28 and SECNA VINST 5239.3.

Confidentiality – The system must ensure the confidentiality of sensitive information by controlling access to information, services, and equipment. Only personnel who have the proper authorization and need-to-know can have access to systems and data. The system must include features and procedures to enforce access control policies for all information, services, and equipment comprising the system.

Integrity – The system must maintain the integrity (i.e., the absence of unauthorized and undetected modification) of information and software while these are processed, stored and transferred across a network or publicly accessible transmission media. Each file or data collection in the system must have an identifiable source throughout its life cycle. Also, the system must ensure the integrity of its mission-critical equipment. Automated and/or manual safeguards must be used to detect and prevent inadvertent or malicious destruction or modification of data.

Availability – The system must protect against denial of service threats. Protection must be proportionate to the operational value of the services and the information provided. This protection must include protection against environmental threats such as loss of power and cooling.

Accountability – The system must support tracing of all security relevant events, including violations and attempted violations of security policy to the individual subsystems and/or users including external connections. The system must enforce the following rules:

1. Personnel and systems connecting to the system must be uniquely identifiable to the system and must have their identities authenticated before being granted access to sensitive information, services, or equipment.

2. Each subsystem handling sensitive or mission-critical information must maintain an audit trail of security relevant events, including attempts by individual users or interfacing subsystems to gain access through interfaces not authorized for that particular purpose. This audit trail must be tamper-resistant and always active.

Assurance – The criticality and sensitivity of the information handled, equipment and services, and the need-to-know of personnel must be identified in order to determine the applicable security requirements. The security implementations chosen must provide adequate security protection commensurate with the criticality of the data, in accordance with the security policy.

Enforcement – The security policy must be enforced throughout the life cycle of the system. All implementations of system security functions including those implemented at the subsystem level must be evaluated to ensure that they adequately enforce the requirements derived from the security policy. Each platform must be evaluated to ensure that the installed system configuration enforces the stated security policy. As a result of this evaluation, an assessment of the vulnerability can be generated. This assessment must be evaluated by the security manager or system administrator to decide if any modifications to the system must be made so that it complies with the security policy. Security best practices must be employed throughout the life cycle of a system to ensure continued compliance with the stated security policy. New system projects must have information security representatives during the planning and preliminary design stages in order to implement security into the design.

✓ INFOSEC Best Practice #3

Create a plan for implementing your security policy.

Once a security policy is established, an implementation plan should be created. Incremental, staged infrastructure improvements and new hires (if any) will help management plan for expenses and create a timetable for implementation.

The implementation plan should include the following steps:

1) Defining implementation guidelines. These guidelines should specify the personnel to receive security alarms and what action is to be taken, chains of command for incident escalation, and reporting requirements.

2) Educating staff, customers, etc. about the security policy.

3) Purchasing any needed hardware/software and hiring any needed personnel.

4) Installing and testing equipment/software.

INFOSEC Network Architecture Design Rules

5.1 PHYSICAL NETWORK SEPARATION

If you are installing a large network, then you may have to create more than one network segment. Practically, if there are a very large number of nodes on an Ethernet network, then separate physical networks must be created. These separate networks can be connected together via a router. Such a large network space increases the risk of network security problems. Therefore, traffic between separate networks must be restricted only to those systems that need to access data. This limited access will decrease the number of users that may compromise each separate physical network.

The Best Practices in this section give guidelines for reducing security risks when dealing with a number of physically separate network segments.

✓ INFOSEC Best Practice #4

Restrict access between separate physical
networks via a filtering router.

A filtering router must be used to restrict access between network
segments. Filtering routers or packet-screening routers control the flow
of IP packets between two or more network segments based on a set of
rules as shown in Figure 5-1. A filtering router has the ability to filter IP
traffic using filtering rules.

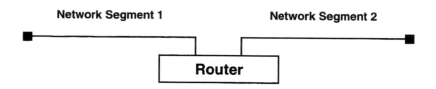

Network Segment 1   **Network Segment 2**

Router

Figure 5-1: Router-based Network Architecture

The network and INFOSEC administrator can set up filtering rules
that specifically allow or disallow IP packets destined for a specific
resource such as a TCP service port (e.g., SMTP mail = port 25, HTTP
= port 80, etc.), or a specific IP address. Therefore, filtering routers
increase security because they restrict traffic between network segments. Access to services and IP addresses can be controlled, thereby
limiting access to an as-needed basis. These filtering routers are one
component of setting up firewalls on a network. Potential intra-corpo-
rate uses are to separate the MIS department or specific research
computers from the rest of the corporate network with access mediated
by filtering rules.

✓ **INFOSEC Best Practice #5**

When there is more than one physical network segment, connect information systems that need to be universally accessible within an organization on a single network segment.

By placing all servers that need to be universally accessible across multiple networks onto a single network segment, users from separate networks can have access to these common systems without opening their own networks to inter-segment traffic. This network access control can be done at the router that connects the individual networks. If performance becomes a problem on the common shared network segment, upgrade the segment to a higher bandwidth.

✓ **INFOSEC Best Practice #6**

Use a switch to isolate traffic between servers, groups of users, and departments.

Use a switch to separate traffic between servers and departments within an organization in order to prevent the unnecessary flow of network traffic throughout an organization. Therefore, if a hacker or internal user starts to monitor the network from a specific PC, then he or she will only have a restricted view of all the packets that are travelling along that specific segment.

5.2 LOGICAL SEPARATION

Another method of restricting access within a single network is to divide the network into separate logical partitions. Each logical partition appears as a separate network, has a separate user accounts database, and has a preconfigured trust relationship between other logical network partitions. Access to resources within a logical network partition is controlled by each domain administrator. Separating the network logically also restricts users from having universal access to all resources on the network and thereby increases information and network security. Typically, one logical network will not be able to access some resources on another logical network unless there is a trust relationship set up between the networks.

The downside is that it requires more work to administer the separate logical partitions. Dividing the network into too many partitions can be inefficient, make it difficult to administer the network, and add more complexity to the network and network security. Typically, there should be a logical separation between large departments or large groups of users. For example, the MIS department may want to have its own logical partition since they need to restrict access to their computers from the general population and would like to have control over additional security on their network. As a practical matter, however, it is much easier to manage a network with a single logical partition having a single accounts database.

 INFOSEC Best Practice #7

Set up logical network separation where you want to increase network security for a group of users.

Set up one or more servers to belong to each logical network partition. Each set of users will be authenticated by a single server in each logical partition and have access only to those resources within it. Logical separation will restrict access to servers by users belonging only to that logical partition and thereby increase security within a single network.

5.3 FIREWALL ARCHITECTURE

Securing your network from the internet and other external communication links requires that your site have a firewall that properly isolates the external network from your internal network. A firewall is a device or collection of devices and software that securely connects a trusted network with an untrusted or public network. Packets must flow past the firewall and be controlled by the firewall by a set of rules that authorize packets to pass between the two networks. Rules are set up at the firewall to enforce the site's security policy.

It is absolutely necessary that your organization's internal network be protected from an external public network such as the internet. The internet is a public network which operates using the TCP/IP protocol. There are millions of connected machines on the network capable of sending mail via SMTP, logging into a computer via telnet, transferring files via FTP, and doing web browsing using HTTP. Connecting to the internet essentially merges your network with the large internet network. In order to be connected your site must establish a connection with an internet service provider (ISP). Connections are established by a leased line, phone line or cable line to the service provider using a modem and for higher speed applications a modem and router (e.g., operating at 56Mbps, 128Mbps, 256Mbps, T1 or some speed in between.).

✔ INFOSEC Best Practice #8

Use a firewall to separate your internal network from the internet.

If you have a network connected via a leased line, DSL or cable connection to the internet, then you will need to use a firewall. DSL and cable modems provide fast connection speeds at inexpensive prices for business or home use, but differ from dial-up modems in that there is a continuous internet connection as long as the PC is turned on. For single PCs connected to the internet in a small office/home office SOHO setting, implement an inexpensive software-based firewall solution that resides on your PC. Inexpensive commercial firewall packages and free public domain software exist specifically to address the DSL and cable modem security problem. These packages can either monitor your PC for intrusion/attack or create a firewall that filters packets according to your own predefined rules.

An organization's internal networks will need to be protected by using a hardware-based firewall solution. SOHO environments can use inexpensive firewall /router hardware that is oriented specifically for the DSL and cable modem market. Businesses that require publicly accessible machines such as mail and web servers will need to implement a firewall with a DMZ (for "demilitarized zone," an area where publicly accessible machines must be located). ISPs may offer their own firewall solutions that can be leased. Filtering routers are often provided and maintained by the ISP as gateways to the internet. It is desirable to have full control of your gateway router so that you do not have an external party controlling access to your organization's network. However, if you do not have the personnel to maintain this device, then an ISP is a good choice. Most large ISPs are security conscious and maintain your router configuration with adequate security.

In order to connect your network to the internet, a gateway computer such as a screening router must be used. The gateway computer is a router that "routes" IP packets between two IP networks (i.e., networks with different IP addresses such as 206.5.94 and 206.5.93). This connection must not allow for the free flow of IP packets between networks, but must filter packets into your network via a set of rules. A screening router will give you this capability. The router must be set up to filter packets not needed for your environment (i.e., FTP, NEWS, FILE, TELNET, any other unnecessary TCP ports). Enable only those ports that you will use.

Filtering routers are used as the gateway and first level of security to the internet. Filtering routers usually have a Unix-based kernel and have filtering software that allows the administrator to create rules that control the filtering of IP packets. Below is an example of rules set up on a filtering router. Most filtering routers do not sit on top of a full operating system, but implement a scaled-down version specifically tailored for the router and security application.

Rule	Direction	Source Address	Destination Address	Protocol	Source Port	Destination Port	Action
1	In	210.150.3.2	210.120.4.3	TCP	1334	25	Permit
2	Out	210.120.4.3	200.150.3.2	TCP	25	1334	Permit
3	Out	210.120.4.3	200.150.3.2	TCP	1441	25	Permit
4	In	200.150.3.2	210.120.4.3	TCP	25	1441	Permit
5	In	15.1.2.4	210.120.4.3	TCP	5250	6150	Deny
6	Out	210.120.4.3	15.1.2.4	TCP	6150	5250	Deny

When configuring a filtering router it is a good idea to turn off all access into your network, then create rules that selectively open up ports that access public services such as email, web pages, and FTP. High-risk TCP/IP services include DNS zone transfers which leak names of internal systems, *tftp* with clear-text passwords, NFS where hackers can read and write files to your system, *rlogin* and *rsh* which require mutually trusting systems, and X-Windows where hackers can monitor user sessions.

 INFOSEC Best Practice #9

Create a perimeter subnet on which all publicly accessible servers must be located.

Any machines to which you want to allow public access (i.e., users on the internet) must be separated from your internal company network. Publicly accessible machines should be placed on a perimeter subnet which is located between your internet gateway and a device (i.e., filtering router, application firewall, etc.) which separates the perimeter subnet from your internal network. By locating all public servers on the perimeter subnet as shown in Figure 5-2a, the public will not have direct access to your internal network, yet will be able to access an organization's servers that are approved for public access. Figure 5-2b shows a router with a built-in perimeter subnet. The perimeter subnet, sometimes called the DMZ, is where publicly accessible machines must be located. These machines are called bastion hosts since they are hardened with security and run applications that will be used by the public. If any of these machines are compromised, then the second router separates the machine

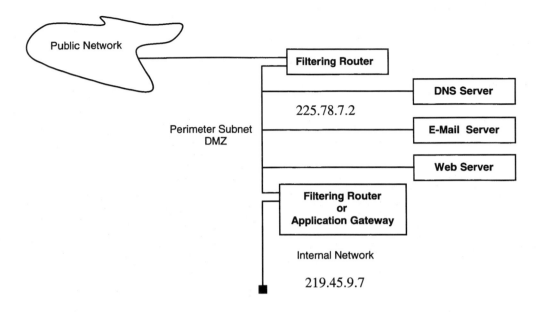

Figure 5-2a: Perimeter Subnet Architecture

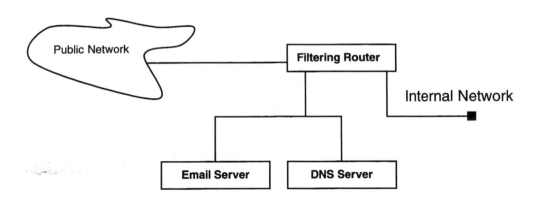

Figure 5-2b: Perimeter Subnet Architecture via Single Filtering

from the internal network. The hacker will only see the perimeter subnet network segment and no other internal traffic.

Mail servers are needed for intranet mail communications within your organization and for sending mail to other organizations over the internet. Since users on the internet can send you mail, locate this mail server on the DMZ and protect this system with extra security measures. Disable FTP on the mail server and set up file protection. For restricted mail communication between known sites, set up secure authentication between servers.

Devote a separate machine to FTP serving. A remote user logs into the FTP server in order to transfer files to or from the server. FTP servers can be attacked by an attacker sending very large files to fill up the disk drive and monopolize the processor. Once a hacker logs into a machine, he will try to probe it for weaknesses. Also, malicious files may be deposited onto the system. Keep this server separate from other public applications.

Set up a separate machine for website serving. Websites are key targets for attack by a hacker. Breaking into a website and posting hacker-composed material is a favorite activity. It is important to secure this machine by using a reasonably secure operating system such as NT or UNIX and to setup file protections. Since this computer is a favorite target, keep your mail system separate.

✓ INFOSEC Best Practice #10

Use a dual-homed application gateway or a filtering router to separate the internal network from the perimeter subnet.

There are many ways one can configure firewalls, the simplest being with a single filtering router and the more secure using multiple machines and a perimeter subnet. The network architecture that needs to be implemented should directly reflect the security policy goals that the company is trying to implement. The security policy will be the result of the acceptable risks and costs that the company is willing to accept and its goals. There are many books on network security that explain in detail how perimeter subnets should be implemented for a variety of scenarios, but it has been my experience that using the above perimeter subnet configuration will result in an acceptable architecture that provides an effective line of defense against attacks. The device that separates the perimeter subnet from your internal company network must be a dual-homed machine (i.e., two separate network cards in a single computer). This device will filter IP traffic between the perimeter subnet and your internal network and will contain separate physical connections to the two network segments. This type of device can be a filtering router or an application gateway that proxies applications. In order to gain access to your internal network, hackers will need to compromise a bastion host and the application gateway machine.

Some firewall software is sold as an application gateway between your internal and external networks. This software replaces the network card driver with its own hardened driver and shuts off all IP traffic between the two networks except that allowed by user-specified rules. It is different from a filtering router in that it is preconfigured with application specific gateways for services such as SMTP, HTTP, FTP, Telnet, and others that it proxies across the two networks. A firewall includes features to configure access to applications such as mail, databases, and virtual private networks (VPN). Also, extensive auditing and alarm features are included, which help log activity, detect suspicious events, and send a message to the network administrator via paging, fax or mail. These firewalls are useful and decrease the chance of misconfiguration of complex filtering router rules. Firewall software packages, however, can be more restrictive than generic IP filtering routers.

 ### INFOSEC Best Practice #11

> Choose a firewall software package that has been favorably reviewed by the NCSA.

The NCSA (National Computer Security Association) conducts tests of firewalls and publishes results. The tests focus on the security features of the firewalls and evaluate their weaknesses. The published results are a good reference for choosing a firewall for your application.

 ### INFOSEC Best Practice #12

> Use a proxy server located on the DMZ to hide the internal IP addresses from external users.

Proxy servers can use two different methods for hiding internal IP addresses and applications. An application-level proxy server runs an instance of an application such as FTP, TELNET, and HTTP to communicate with the external hosts and an instance of the application for communication with internal systems. A circuit-level proxy server has a copy of TCP for the internal network and a copy for the external network.

The proxy server transfers data between the two instances of the application. The systems administrator must decide what type of proxy application to implement based on performance, cost, and security requirements.

Proxy servers are very CPU intensive so a dedicated computer with adequate CPU power should be used. Proxy servers have extensive monitoring software and alarms that can page, fax or phone an individual if suspicious activity takes place across or on the proxying firewall. To increase security of your internal network, all internal IP addresses can be hidden from the external network by being mapped to a proxy server address. In order to exploit weaknesses most attackers try to discover IP addresses of internal machines. IP address hiding will make it more difficult for the hacker to discover the address. If you have an existing TCP/IP network, however, converting your IPs to unknown, private IPs can be a large task. It is recommended that Class C licenses be used for all internal machines. By hiding internal IP addresses, hackers cannot directly aim their attack at a specific, known internal IP address. Other, more secure machines, need to be compromised in order to gain access to the network.

✔ INFOSEC Best Practice #13

Filter out incoming packets from the Internet that have source addresses belonging to the internal network.

Internal source addresses that arrive from the external network are obviously not from the inside and therefore should be filtered out by the filtering router.

✔ INFOSEC Best Practice #14

Block all IP traffic into the internal network except from authorized sources.

The filtering firewall should block addresses that are not authorized to access your site. This is not possible if you have a web site, mail or FTP server where the public must have access, but should be done for any traffic between the DMZ and the internal network. Start by blocking out everyone and then open up specific IPs to the internal network that need access.

✔ INFOSEC Best Practice #15

Filter out incoming packets to turned off TCP ports.

Most TCP ports are not used on a machine with TCP/IP capability. The filtering router between your internal and external network should filter out all port traffic except that which is authorized for applications such as web service (port 80), mail service (port 25), POP3 traffic (port 110), FTP service (port 21 for commands, data port is negotiated), and any other ports that are used for database access and secure transactions.

✔ INFOSEC Best Practice #16

Allow outbound, but no inbound, TELNET sessions.

A TELNET session allows a user to login into a computer. If that computer is not secured by information security measures, then there is a good chance that the logged-in user can cause damage to the system. If it is an internal system, then an unauthorized hacker can exploit weaknesses to your internal systems. If you must have a TELNET session into your network, either locate it on the DMZ or have a dial-in connection to a standalone system that is not connected to the network.

✔ INFOSEC Best Practice #17

Log all firewall events.

All firewall components should have audit software that can assist in the recognition and prevention of penetration attempts. Logging should be turned on and all logs should be archived.

✔ INFOSEC Best Practice #18

Audit the firewall.

Over time, firewall computers may need modifications, such as operating system service pack updates (i.e., patches), application software upgrades and or service packs, and other system activity. Sometimes, these updates of software open up security holes that did not exist before. More often these updates repair security problems, but given the complexity of code unexpected problems can arise. On a periodic basis, the firewall should be audited to determine whether it is meeting its security objectives.

✓ **INFOSEC Best Practice #19**

Do not connect computers with extremely sensitive information to the internet, even indirectly using a firewall.

Typically, information such as certain MIS financial data and corporate secrets (e.g., confidential processes, formulas, trade secrets, etc.) must be restricted. The risk of exposure of such data versus the benefits of having an internet connection must be weighed and a risk/benefit matrix constructed. In some cases, such as military secret data or some corporate and bank information, the information must *never* be compromised. In these cases, it is safer to remove that information from any network connection that is directly or indirectly connected to the internet. Operating systems that are classified as secure at levels C2 or B1 and firewalls may have unknown holes that might be exploited by hackers. There is never a 100% assurance that these systems are secure. Also, even though the operating system or firewall software may be adequately secure, it can be misconfigured by the MIS staff and thereby inadvertently open up holes into your network. When service patches are installed to the operating system, the threat is reduced by the new fixes. However, these patches may sometimes inadvertently increase the threat by introducing new holes that were not there previously. The organization should determine the risk that is acceptable for having information on the internet and assume that a system can be broken into. Information that is sensitive but needs to be disseminated must be encrypted on the computer and during communication between machines.

5.4 WAN-BASED NETWORK ARCHITECTURE

Wide Area Network (WAN) connections to your LAN are usually dedicated network links such as ISDN, 56 Kbps, T1, fractional T1, DSL, cable or dial-up POTS modem connections between a hub site and multiple remote sites. These communication links are usually connected via a router or modem to your network and appear as a transparent part of your network. Also, in-bound dial-up modem links can use a remote access service that connects the remote computers to your network as if it were local and allows access to your authorized network resources.

✔ INFOSEC Best Practice #20

Locate all WAN connections on a central hub that is separated from public communication links by a firewall.

Connect all your WAN segments from multiple sites within your organization to a router located behind your firewall on the internal network as shown in Figure 5-3. It is very important that the external sites do not have their own public network connection since WAN links

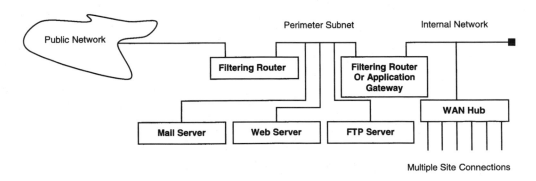

Figure 5-3: WAN Architecture

connect internal networks together, bypassing the firewall. For sites that do not have dedicated network connections and use dial-up lines, then those connections must come into the site's modem server which is also located on the internal network. Do not locate the WAN hub on the DMZ since it would require opening up too many ports on the firewall in order for remote users to access internal resources.

 INFOSEC Best Practice #21

Use a single Internet connection for a WAN.

Multiple access points to the Internet throughout an organization offer multiple points of entry for the hacker. Multiple access points are usually maintained by different personnel at various locations and vary in their enforcement of an organization's security policy. Therefore, a single public connection with a firewall, DMZ, and bastion host servers for mail, FTP, and web will be more likely to be properly protected using a security policy. If an organization is very large, then multiple points of access to a public network may have to be used to enhance performance and allow for practical maintenance and update of the site.

5.5 MODEM SERVER NETWORK ARCHITECTURE

A modem is used for dialing into an organization from remote locations during travel or from home. A connection is established when a user dials in over a phone line to a modem in order to connect to a computer, logon, and access some internal application or service. Some users may also use modems to establish a dial-out connection to an external computer. These types of connections are decreasing because of the internet.

If your site needs to maintain modems for this type of activity, then a dedicated modem server must be used for dialing into and out of the internal network. Do not overlook securing the modem server, since it is often used as a backdoor by hackers to gain access to your network.

✓ INFOSEC Best Practice #22

Do not allow any modems on individual machines.

Install all modems on a modem server that is administered by the organization's system manager. Modems on individual machines are very high security risks. Hackers may use these modems to dial into your network, bypassing your network security (i.e., the firewall). Those users that require modems on their individual machines should not be connected to your network.

✓ INFOSEC Best Practice #23

Locate modem servers on the internal network.

Users dial into an internal network to access resources such as email; therefore, the modem server must be located on your internal network. Since the modem server is located on the internal network it must be secured at the level of a bastion host and the user must be authenticated. Sometimes users are careless in divulging their modem numbers to people outside an organization. Sometimes an organization publishes numbers freely in newsletters. Hackers use this information to try to bypass the firewall by dialing into a non-secured machine inside your firewall. Therefore, keep modem numbers confidential. Do not locate the modem server on the perimeter subnet since you will need to open up ports through your firewall to allow users access to internal resources. These holes in the firewall are additional points of weakness that can be exploited by a hacker.

5.6 VIRTUAL PRIVATE NETWORK SECURITY

✔ INFOSEC Best Practice #24

Use a Virtual Private Network (VPN) over the internet between two sites in place of a leased line connection for less sensitive site-to-site communications.

Virtual Private Networks (VPNs) allow for secure connections between sites across the internet. These are a less expensive way of secure communication between sites as compared to point-to-point or frame relay WAN communication. The VPN is an encrypted session between two trusted hosts and can be accomplished by using routers or application machines with the same encryption and software. The drawback of this technique is that a public network is used to transmit potentially sensitive information even though it is encrypted. Using the internet will not guarantee delivery of the data, but encryption will ensure privacy. Also, using an encrypted tunnel through the firewall bypasses security and therefore both connecting sites must not overlook the security of their systems and user access.

5.7 HUBS

 INFOSEC Best Practice #25

Use hubs to isolate traffic in order to make it more
difficult for hackers to perform sniffing of the network.

Using a hub to isolate traffic between areas on the network will
make it more difficult for a hacker to build a complete picture of your
entire network by sniffing packets. (Sniffing refers to a passive attack
where a hacker observes network traffic without disturbing it.) Active
hubs used in 10-Base-T configurations forward packets only intended
for each system on the hub, therefore making promiscuous sniffing
useless.

Rules for Selecting Security Hardware and Software

A wide variety of security hardware and software is currently available, from numerous vendors. Selecting the correct equipment and software to fit your security needs is a crucial step in configuring a security system. This chapter discusses three important rules to consider.

✓ **INFOSEC Best Practice #26**

> Select network and security hardware and software from vendors with established product lines.

Security hardware and security software should be purchased from reputable manufacturers that have established product lines. New products may have bugs in them that can unintentionally compromise the security of a system. Do not get first releases of products, unless you have no other alternative to solving your problem.

INFOSEC Best Practice #27

Select hardware and software from vendors that support standards and that offer new products at the forefront of technology.

Standards are very important when it comes to security. In order to implement encryption and authentication schemes that will be compatible with future products, standards should be followed. Very specific intra-organizational communications can use non-standards-based products (i.e., encryption devices), but it is not recommended. Generally, not complying with standards will hurt you in the long run.

INFOSEC Best Practice #28

Select hardware and software from vendors that have dedicated support staffs with knowledgeable engineers.

Poor support from a vendor can lead to security problems. To evaluate a company's technical staff, call them to get your questions answered about your hardware selection and evaluate their level of knowledge.

Physical Security Rules

Physical security involves limiting access to computer hardware, wiring, displays, and network devices. Your security policy must address it in order to prevent accidents, damage or tampering of physical hardware. The following set of best practices provide a set of guidelines for increasing physical security.

7.1 COMPUTERS

The most obvious component of physical security is the computer itself. This collection of best practices stresses steps that can be taken to protect the machines from a variety of risks.

✔ **INFOSEC Best Practice #29**

Locate all server computer hardware for mission-critical systems in a secure location that is locked and restricted to authorized personnel.

Server computers usually service departments or groups of users. These systems must be located in secure, restricted areas to limit the possibility of a user accidentally shutting off the machine, damaging it by spilling a liquid on it, or seeing sensitive passwords or data. Open rooms provide an opportunity for malicious users to copy sensitive data onto portable media (i.e., floppies, tapes, CDs) or plant viruses on the server. Combination locks, keyed entry, or access cards must secure each entrance. Backup keys must be kept in a locked cabinet located in a secured room.

 ## INFOSEC Best Practice #30

Use an air conditioning system in rooms where server computers are located.

Rooms with server computers must have proper air conditioning and humidity control. Air conditioning units located in the server room minimize the impact from building related HVAC events. Computers and other related hardware have temperature and humidity operational ranges. If the ranges are exceeded, then these systems can fail.

 ## INFOSEC Best Practice #31

Servers must have uninterruptable power supplies.

Surge suppressors and uninterruptable power supplies (UPS) will eliminate power surges along power lines and reduce downtime due to brown outs. UPSs are becoming relatively inexpensive and should be considered for desktop systems as well.

✔ INFOSEC Best Practice #32

Install fire protection systems in rooms where mission-critical servers are located.

Systems that impact business operations must have fire control systems installed in event of a fire. These systems must not be water-based, but be halon-based to quickly eliminate oxygen supply during an electrical fire. A fire that destroys hardware can severely impact an organization. Setting up a new facility with security controls takes a very long time.

✔ INFOSEC Best Practice #33

Use true floor to ceiling walls in rooms where mission-critical server computers are located.

Computers such as MIS systems with an organization's accounting data or systems with confidential databases must be located in rooms with restricted access that cannot be circumvented via access through the ceiling or vents.

INFOSEC Best Practice #34

Locate computers with top-secret information in a room with "Tempest" shielding.

Government sites that have top secret information or very select corporate sites where corporate espionage is suspected should have "Tempest" shielding. This shielding prevents detection of electromagnetic signals from keystrokes and messages displayed on the video monitor from being captured by unauthorized people with highly specialized equipment.

 INFOSEC Best Practice #35

Maintain a disaster recovery plan for your organization's computer facilities.

If there is a catastrophe and your organization's computers need to be replaced, then a contingency plan or disaster recovery plan should be in place on how to accomplish this goal. Having third party resources that can be leased to run your organization's software needs to be considered. The disaster recovery plan must take into consideration your INFOSEC Best Practices since a disaster can provide a period where hackers can break into your network when your facility is in transition. Also, third party facilities must be researched on how they support information security.

7.2 WIRING

 INFOSEC Best Practice #36

Locate the network backbone in conduits or protected areas.

The network backbone wiring must be located in conduits or areas not accessible to the general public. Access points to the backbone must be located in phone closets or other installed cabinets that are secured by a lock. Avoid running backbone wiring along hallways where the general public has access. If your backbone is maliciously tampered with, your entire segment can be brought down. This is also advisable for departmental hub wiring.

Network devices such as repeaters, routers, and hubs must be placed in locked areas. Placing them in open areas invites problems with intentional or unintentional tampering with the device. People are curious and will be drawn to these devices. Problems may be rare, but when they do arise it may be difficult to find the problem and it will affect a lot of people on the network.

 INFOSEC Best Practice #37

Approve all new wiring additions and connections through an approval process.

In order to install new wiring at a site or new nodes in a wireless network, approval from the organization's IT department must be granted. Departments or individuals must not be allowed to add computers or make modifications to the network. Departments that try to independently add wiring may inadvertently bring down the segment. Adding computers to the network will require assignment of available ports on a hub. Also, the wiring must be exactly matched to the existing wiring. If category 5 wiring is used, then all ports to a hub should have category 5. Finally, allowing corporate users to add their own computers to unofficial network segments can cause IP conflicts.

 INFOSEC Best Practice #38

> Install wiring that can support the fastest transmission speed available.

Network technologies are rapidly increasing computer bandwidth. At this writing, Ethernet speed is at 10 Mbps, Fast Ethernet is at 100 Mbps, and greater throughput is being introduced via new technologies at a fast pace. Supporting these fast transmission speeds requires adequate wiring. Physical wiring is labor intensive to install, but is in itself inexpensive. Buy the best wire you can at the time of installation to increase the longevity of the network infrastructure.

 INFOSEC Best Practice #39

> Document your network configuration, including the layout of your wiring and all network devices.

Documenting a site's wiring and network configuration is the last thing that network managers want to do. It is however, extremely important to keep documentation, preferably graphic drawings, of your network layout and the devices that are attached to it. As networks expand it is very easy to forget what the configuration is and where various network hardware is located. As personnel come and go, the company must maintain documentation that can be passed on to new network managers. When problems arise, the documentation can save you a tremendous amount of time in troubleshooting the network.

 INFOSEC Best Practice #40

Fiber optic or wireless technology must be used for connections between buildings.

To avoid problems of coupling with stray currents such as lightning and motors, use fiber optic cabling or wireless connections between buildings. Fiber optic cable cannot couple with electromagnetic fields or stray currents because it is made of silica (i.e., material used to make glass). Also, fiber optic cable cannot be easily tapped, thereby reducing the chance of unauthorized nodes or devices being placed on your network. Also, shielded wiring (e.g., coaxial cable, shielded twisted pair) for computer networks will reduce the chance of picking up stray currents. Wireless connections are less reliable, easy to install, and do not provide a physical media that can be tapped. However, wireless connections should be encrypted since the signal is transmitted into the open and can be picked up by other unauthorized means.

7.3 COMPUTER CONSOLES

 INFOSEC Best Practice #41

Locate computer consoles for mission-critical computers in secure rooms.

Consoles attached to servers and other mission-critical machines are used by system administrators to perform system maintenance that requires full access to system resources and data. If the network and server management software is secure enough, then management of these machines can be done remotely. Locating these consoles in secure rooms will prevent inadvertent or malicious access by unauthorized users and will reduce the chance of system passwords being seen during keyboard entry.

7.4 NETWORK DEVICES

 INFOSEC Best Practice #42

Restrict physical access to network devices to a level determined by a risk index.

Use the risk index specified in Best Practice #1 to determine whether network devices should be placed in a locked cabinet, a hidden area, such as a ceiling, or in an open location.

7.5 DATA SECURITY

✓ **INFOSEC Best Practice #43**

Keep all tape, floppy, and optical disk backups of mission-critical computers and sensitive data in a secure room.

Computers may contain private and financial data for many individuals, projects, departments, divisions, etc. Tape, floppy, and CD backups of those systems must be stored in a room with the same level of access security as the servers on which the media was created. The data on the backups is the same as that which resides on the computer. If the data is sensitive, then it should have the same level of security protection as the computer on which it is stored. In all cases it must always be stored in a locked room.

✓ **INFOSEC Best Practice #44**

Store backup media for mission-critical computers either off-site, in another building, on a separate floor or in a separate room.

Data can be backed up on tapes, CD-ROMs or ZIP or floppy disks. Mission-critical data necessary to keep your company running must be stored off-site. Project specific servers must have their data stored in a separate building or a separate room from where the computers reside. Finally, archived personal data on PCs and workstations must be stored in a departmental or corporate archive room. Day to day data can be stored within the office. It is important that the criticality of the data be associated with a risk index that determines where to store the data. In some cases all data at a site will need to be stored off-site and in other cases on-site storage will be sufficient due to economic or low-risk reasons. The risk index will be company specific based on the importance each company puts on specific types of data. Separating your data from the site at which it is backed up is a common practice in the event of fire, natural disaster, or accidents.

 ## INFOSEC Best Practice #45

> Access security to your backup storage facility must be equivalent to the access security to the computer room where the data is present.

All backup storage facilities must have controlled access. The data on the backup tapes is more vulnerable than when it resides on the computer. Data stored on the computer is protected by operating system security such as file protection and access control. Also, the data resides on a hard disk which is difficult to remove out of the computer. However, when that data is on tape, an unauthorized person can use software that can understand the tape format (i.e., ASCII, EBCDIC, NT Backup, VMS backup, UNIX tar, UNIX cpio, etc.). If the data is encrypted on tape, then it will be difficult to decipher. However, most corporate data is not encrypted and can be read by the appropriate backup encoding software and then interpreted by the appropriate application program (Lotus, MS Word, etc.). This is an area of security that is often overlooked at organizations.

INFOSEC Best Practice #46

Control the distribution of software and only allow authorized software on site.

This is a time-consuming process and is difficult to implement since software can be easily copied from the internet without going through a corporate approval process. A database of all software purchased should be maintained by the organization and tagged to a computer. Each computer should have an identification tag and all software should have an identification number. Software is available on the market that does software tracking on your network and maintains the software status of each machine in a database. These programs cost money, but can simplify the process of software tracking. By having such a process in place, the company can show that it is committed to keeping track of all software in the event that the company is audited. Also, unauthorized software from ambiguous sources can be eliminated from your network. Hackers often use security holes in software packages to gain access to the operating system. Keeping unnecessary or unauthorized software off of an organization's computers will reduce the possibility of security breaches.

INFOSEC Best Practice #47

Destroy floppy disks, tapes and optical media that contain sensitive data and are no longer used.

Do not reuse storage media containing sensitive data. Destroy media that is no longer used. The sensitivity of data on old storage media may be forgotten and data disposed of carelessly.

Network hardware security is used to restrict access to software configurable hardware. The network hardware addressed are firewall computers, routers, switches, printers, and modem servers.

Network Hardware Security

This section addresses best practices for dealing with security of the network hardware, including screening routers/firewall computers, switches, printers, adapter cards, and modems.

8.1 FIREWALL COMPUTERS

By definition, a firewall is a network security device, a combination of hardware and software, that prevents unauthorized users from accessing an intranet or LAN. There are numerous types of firewall schemes: packet filtering routers, screening routers, embedded firewall, etc., all at various levels of cost and complexity.

No matter what firewall scheme is employed, there are specific security measures that apply in all cases.

✓ **INFOSEC Best Practice #48**

Standardize on screening router hardware and software.

Screening routers must be the same throughout a site so that the network administrator can easily configure the machines without an increased chance of making a mistake when defining rules. Also, in order for sites to communicate using encryption, such as during an encrypted VPN connection, routers at both ends of the communication link must have the same encryption hardware or algorithm. Software revisions can take place on all routers at the same time rather than piecemeal. Also, having the same software revision level on router hardware will reduce the chance of unexpected incompatibilities.

 INFOSEC Best Practice #49

All routers must have operating systems with at least C2 level security.

Commercial routers run a small kernel operating system usually derived from UNIX and designed to be secure. However, PCs can be turned into routers using software that can be purchased. These PCs must have operating systems that have at least C2 level security capability (as described in the National Computer Security Center's Rainbow series Orange Book, *Trusted Computer Standards Evaluation Criteria*), so that they can be adequately secured against malicious tampering.

 INFOSEC Best Practice #50

Select routers that support the filtering of all protocols used within an organization.

There may be many protocols operating in an organization (e.g., TCP/IP, IPX, NetBios, etc.) that must be supported by the routers that are used. Filtering routers that allow the security administrator to determine which packets pass the router and which don't should have the capability to act separately on the different protocols. Choose a router that supports all your current and anticipated protocols.

✓ **INFOSEC Best Practice #51**

> Standardize on computer hardware and software for application level gateways.

Standardizing on computer hardware and software for application gateways (e.g., firewalls that proxy POP3, SMTP, HTTP, FTP, etc.) makes it easier for the system administrator to know the particular hardware platform and software in more detail and thereby secure the system more effectively. This should include operating system, web server, mail server, proxy server, and firewall software. However, if there is a hole to be exploited and a hacker finds it, he or she can exploit it for all your systems.

8.2 SWITCHES

Switches are used to isolate traffic on the network backbone, can be assigned an IP address and be managed remotely by protocols such as SNMP. When an IP is assigned and the hardware is software configurable, then it is subject to attack by hackers. A switch usually supports a large department or many departments spread across several buildings. Also, switches are replacing older style Ethernet backbones by segmenting traffic and are therefore very important network devices that need to be protected by network security best practices.

 INFOSEC Best Practice #52

> If a problem is suspected, then run internal diagnostics on the switch.

If there is a major problem with a network device, then diagnostics must be run to analyze the device for hardware problems. If there is a configuration problem, then it may be security related. Expensive switches will not usually have a spare backup, but must be sent back to the manufacturer to be replaced. Reputable manufacturers of these types of network devices will normally send you a working unit overnight.

 INFOSEC Best Practice #53

> Switches that are software configurable must have access restricted by a password.

Switches that are configurable or managed over the network must have access control via a password. The network administrator must change this password immediately after giving the device an IP address. SNMP-managed devices (simple network management protocol) must have obscure names in order to make it more difficult for a hacker to use SNMP to obtain and alter network device configuration. Information security best practices for selecting the password must be followed.

8.3 PRINTERS

 INFOSEC Best Practice #54

Printers that are software configurable must have access restricted by a password.

Some network printers can be configured over the network and therefore must be password protected. The password must not be the default password assigned to the system from the factory and must only be known to the system administrator. Hackers will first try using factory default passwords to try to break into the printer server device and disable printing for a network. Information security best practices for selecting the password must be followed.

8.4 NETWORK ADAPTERS

 INFOSEC Best Practice #55

Install non-promiscuous network interfaces on PC computers.

Since PCs do not have the same physical or operating system security as server computers, install network interfaces (i.e., network adapter cards) that do not support promiscuous mode. Check the vendor specification when selecting this hardware. Hackers can use network adapters with promiscuous mode, which allows the card to capture ALL packets flowing on the cable to which it is connected.

8.5 MODEM SECURITY

The goal of modem security is to provide a wall between the modem-based external link and the internal network.

 INFOSEC Best Practice #56

Place modems on a dedicated server.

Modems must not be scattered throughout an organization on individual PCs or internal servers. Modems are a potential backdoor into an internal network that bypass firewall security. Modems are placed on the internal network and not the DMZ in order not to have to open holes in the firewall that allow users communication with the dial-out or dial-in modems. It is extremely important that this best practice be enforced since this is a frequently used method by hackers to break into a network. People may give out their modem number to all kinds of people, not realizing the consequences. Place modems on a dedicated modem server that is in a secured location. Placing modems in a secure location will prevent unauthorized users from altering microcode, passwords (used for remote configuration), and modem switches.

 INFOSEC Best Practice #57

Keep your modem telephone numbers private.

Modem telephone numbers should be treated similarly to passwords since this is the type of information that hackers are looking for to find a backdoor into your network. Do not post modem telephone numbers on your webserver, do not distribute phone numbers via email or hardcopy distribution, and do not keep them in electronic files located on your servers. Divulge passwords only to those users that need to use them for dialing into the network from their laptops during travel or from home.

✓ INFOSEC Best Practice #58

Require a minimum authentication at the server of a username and password when dialing into the modem server.

Authenticate users that are dialing into the network by using a username and password. These users are logging into a computer remotely and must follow the same authentication process.

✓ INFOSEC Best Practice #59

Require the use of a modem communication protocol that has encryption.

A modem communication protocol such as Microsoft RAS (Remote Access Server) should be used that has built-in authentication protocols and encryption capability (MD4). When two sites want to communicate securely and ensure the privacy of data either over a POTS, ISDN or internet connection, encryption should be used. Another option when on the internet, is to use a point-to-point tunneling protocol with encryption over the IP transport mechanism.

INFOSEC Best Practice #60

Set dial-in and dial-out permissions for each user.

Most server operating systems allow the administrator of the machine to configure dial-in and dial-out permissions when setting up the security policy for groups of users. For each group of users the security policy in your account management program should have the option of restricting access to your modem server. If desired, restrict dial-in access by time of day. As a default, the policy must have callback turned off and access control turned on. Users that travel or work from home and need to connect to corporate mail systems or file systems will need to have dial-in permissions granted. Grant these on an as-needed basis only. Therefore, hackers will have a much smaller set of accounts to break into.

 INFOSEC Best Practice #61

Log all dial-in and dial-out events to a file.

Keep a log file of all dial-in and dial-out events. The security administrator can analyze the log file by scanning it manually or with security analyzer software. Suspicious activity can alert the security administrator to change an account password and/or username.

✓ **INFOSEC Best Practice #62**

Do not allow laptops with wireless modems into restricted computer facilities.

Confidential data can be sent to unauthorized sources without a trace when using a cellular modem. Networks where highly sensitive data resides must not allow such devices to connect, since it can be possible to copy sensitive data from a resource on the network, establish a new wireless dial-out connection that bypasses security, and transfer data out of the facility.

 INFOSEC Best Practice #63

Log all modem server connections.

The modem server must log all modem connections including who connected, time of connection, length of session, and destination ID or phone number. This log should be reviewed by the system administrator to look for suspicious activity. If suspicious activity is found, then the account should be disabled and the user of the account contacted.

 INFOSEC Best Practice #64

Standalone PCs that have modems must be configured using the security guidelines of a bastion host machine.

A standalone PC that has a modem will not have a filtering router separating it from the public connection. These PCs should have anti-virus software and be configured with some of the security guidelines of a bastion host machine. An operating system such as Microsoft NT or UNIX must be used. Also, inexpensive software is available for PCs that monitors the connection for attack. This security software must be used for PCs that have static IP addresses (e.g., DSL or cable modem connections).

 ### INFOSEC Best Practice #65

Allow dial-in permissions only for those users that need remote access.

Some dial-in software allows the administrator to set modem dial-in permissions for users. This is a level of access control that will permit only those users that have been authorized by the administrator to dial into the network. Keep dial-in permissions as restrictive as possible. If dial-in permission is granted, then authentication by username and password must follow.

 ### INFOSEC Best Practice #66

Use encrypted authentication for your dial-in software.

Encrypted authentication such as RSA MD4 should be used in order not to send any clear-text passwords. This encrypted authentication should be enabled by the administrator when configuring the dial-in software for your modem server.

 ### INFOSEC Best Practice #67

Locate modem servers for public access on the DMZ.

If you have resources that need to be accessed by the public using a modem, then locate these modems on the perimeter subnet (i.e., DMZ). If public modems are maintained for bulletin boards or for some other purpose, then these modems must not have access to any internal resources. Also, do not open up any ports on the firewall to allow access to internal resources.

Operating System Security Rules

This section addresses best practices for setting up security within operating systems. Authentication, file protection, virus checking, file sharing, network software, and security logging are discussed.

9.1 TRUSTED OPERATING SYSTEMS

Trusted operating systems have security features built into the operating system. The National Computer Security Center's Rainbow series Orange Book, *Trusted Computer Standards Evaluation Criteria* describes several levels of trust including C1, C2, B1, B2, and B3. Currently, there are no commercial operating systems that have been certified beyond B1. These B1 operating systems are used primarily by the government. To secure systems with any level of confidence, operating systems that are capable of C2 or B1 security should be used in your network environment.

9.1.1 B1 Trusted Operating Systems

B1 level trusted operating systems are considerably more expensive than C2 level operating systems because they are used in very selective markets. As the commercial segment begins to deploy these operating systems in greater numbers, the price should come down. Currently, B1 operating systems should be used for government and military applications that need to transmit sensitive, but not secret, data and for commercial banking, financial services, and other commercial applications where security and confidentiality are very important.

9.2 AUTHENTICATION

✓ INFOSEC Best Practice #68

All server operating systems must have a minimum of a C2 level of trust.

C2 is a government designation for computer security that requires computers to have the ability to control access to the computer via usernames and passwords, and protect files by assigning ownership and access rights. Desktop operating systems are recommended to have at least C2 compliance to protect individual systems from unauthorized access. Without these features the data on a computer system is vulnerable to anyone having access to the physical system. Some versions of operating systems have most of the C2 features yet are not C2 compliant. This may be acceptable upon review of the missing features. Most systems such as UNIX and NT can be configured to meet C2 compliance. C2, however, is somewhat dated and has many limitations. Securing most server based operating systems will require going beyond C2 compliance with configuration and protection as specified in the Best Practices outlined in this manual. The government also has more stringent security designations such as B1, B2, and B3. Mission-critical server operating systems may need to have B2 compliance. These security levels address the carrying of classification tags on all data. Data objects are tagged with a classification level such as secret, classified, confidential and unclassified. Access to these data objects is available only to other objects that carry the correct classification level. This type of classification scheme may also be applied to corporate data with differing levels of sensitivity.

✓ INFOSEC Best Practice #69

Username and password authentication must be used to access desktop computers.

Username and password authentication must be used to logon to server and desktop computer systems (Reference Green Book "Department of Defense Password Management Guideline" CSC-STD-002-85). Installing an operating system with this access control capability will allow the user to secure the computer when not in use and prevent illegal entry onto the system.

✓ INFOSEC Best Practice #70

Use one-time password generation hardware or software to authenticate users for access to systems with mission-critical data.

Systems that have sensitive corporate data must authenticate users with one-time passwords generated by handheld devices or software such as S/Key. S/Key requires that the remote host know a password that will not be transmitted over an insecure channel. When you connect to the host, you get a challenge response. The challenge information and password that you know plug into an algorithm that generates the appropriate response to the challenge from the remote host. The algorithm-generated response should match the challenge response if the password is the same on both sides. Thus, the password is never sent over the network, and the challenge is never used twice.

Hardware authenticators should be PIN/Synchronous and require keying in a PIN by the user to the authenticator device that then produces a password as a function of its internal clock. The user then enters the generated password into the computer system. This type of system authenticates the user in possession of the handheld authenticator and limits eavesdropping of passwords to non-network means. It increases security by requiring the user to know a password and additionally to carry an authenticator that usually has a limited distribution. Handheld authenticators should be kept in a secure area and issued to people only when they need to use the system and then returned after use. As an alternative to the handheld authenticator, a smart card can be used which requires entering a PIN into the smart card followed by generation of a one-time password. Interaction with the computer takes place via a smart card reader that doesn't require the user to enter the generated password. This may be done at initial login only, if multiple personnel use the machine.

✔ **INFOSEC Best Practice #71**

Use biometric authentication for systems that hold highly sensitive information.

Some systems with very sensitive or government classified data may require the use of a biometric device as the first step in a multilevel authentication process. A biometric device requires authentication of the user by scanning a physical attribute as proof of identity. Examples of biometric devices are fingerprint, retina scanners, handprint, and facial feature devices. These devices are all coming down in price, which make them more attractive for a variety of applications. This type of authentication requires the individual's presence and cannot be circumvented as easily as stolen smart cards or passwords.

As an example, a smart card can hold information about a person such as fingerprint, photo, and other identifying information. When a user desires access to a closed area or to a computer, a smart card is scanned, the fingerprint is scanned, and compared to what is on the card. If there is a match, then access is granted. Photos and other descriptive information are useful when there is a human guard that provides another level of check. This is useful for very secure environments such as airports.

✔ **INFOSEC Best Practice #72**

Expire passwords after a designated period of time.

Your corporate security policy should specify a schedule indicating how often each user's password must be changed. This schedule must be incorporated into the security policy for user accounts so that all user account passwords expire after a designated period. It is very important that user accounts *not* have a "never expire" flag set. Users do not want to change passwords often and system administrators do not want to be bothered about password expiration problems. Therefore, setting a sensible expiration password expiration policy increases the security of your system. Examples of periods often used for password expiration are 60 days and 90 days. The policy for expiration must be linked to the type of environment within an organization. For example, if there is a large turnover of personnel or temporary accounts that are granted on the system, then the expiration of passwords should be shorter as compared to systems with relatively few accounts and no organizational turnover.

 INFOSEC Best Practice #73

Use "pass phrases" or a mix of letters and numbers for passwords.

Passwords must NOT include the following:

a. a portion or variation of an account username,

b. a portion or variation of your real name, address or phone number,

c. words or variations of words in a dictionary,

d. words or variations of foreign words,

e. words spelled backward,

f. repeated character strings,

g. only numeric digits,

h. only alphabetic characters,

i. passwords less than six alphanumeric characters.

The weakest point in security is usually the password. People choose short, easy-to-remember passwords that they do not change often. Passwords must ideally consist of a mix of characters and numbers interspersed in a long cryptic sequence (i.e., k3k5k*&eklx!!!i0). This is too difficult to remember, therefore using a long phrase that is meaningful to you personally is a good alternative. This may be a code which has meaning for a user, such as "My real age is 43" or "I have 6 pointy-haired bosses."

✓ INFOSEC Best Practice #74

Check passwords against a password history file.

Sophisticated operating systems such as UNIX and Microsoft NT contain a user account option for maintaining a history of used passwords. The program will not let a user reuse an old password for a designated period of time. Therefore, the user must use new passwords that nobody else will know or remember.

✓ **INFOSEC Best Practice #75**

Enforce a minimum password length of at least six alphanumeric characters.

Most user account management programs allow the administrator to enforce a minimum length for a password. The longer the password, the less chance that a password cracking program will find your password. Most password cracking programs generate combinations of letters and numbers to create a password that is used to try to break into an account. The longer the password and the more characters that are used, the more difficult it is to crack it. A seven-letter word has 24^7 combinations, if letters are used, and 34^7 combinations if both letters and numbers are used. Each of those passwords has to be tried against an account on the system. However, it is possible that the password program will generate your password early in the password generation process. Using a phrase for your password makes it difficult to crack your password.

✓ **INFOSEC Best Practice #76**

Automatically disable the user account if there are more than six bad login attempts.

An attack on a user account will use a program that generates passwords one at a time against a user account until it successfully logs into the system. This usually requires many passwords to be tried, unless a common password is used. Most operating systems have an account security feature that can be set by the system administrator to automatically disable an account after a designated number of login attempts. This flag is often set to disable the account after about six unsuccessful login attempts. It is highly unlikely that the user will enter their password incorrectly that many times. When the account is disabled only the administrator will be able to enable the account again. If an attack is actually occurring, the administrator must change the user name of the account and make sure the user selects a satisfactory password. A message must be sent to all users on the system warning users that attacks are occurring on the machine and that their passwords may have to be changed to comply with security guidelines.

✓ INFOSEC Best Practice #77

Use Kerberos authentication in highly vulnerable environments.

Kerberos is a network security protocol that uses strong encryption and a complex ticket-granting algorithm to authenticate users on a network and to allow encrypted data streams over an IP network. Some TCP/IP communication protocols such as FTP and TELNET transmit user IDs and passwords in clear text. Kerberos is a good solution in environments such as universities where other security mechanisms are difficult to implement and enforce and where the environment needs to be open. It is difficult to set up, but is becoming more ubiquitous and will be distributed in conventional operating systems.

9.3 ACCOUNT SECURITY

✓ INFOSEC Best Practice #78

Do not disclose a computer's identity until login is completed successfully.

Set up the operating system so that the system login screen does not identify the computer system by name or function until after login is complete. Unauthorized personnel do not need to know the identity of machines unless they need to use them. Hackers find this type of information valuable since it may identify valuable targets to break into.

✓ INFOSEC Best Practice #79

Use an automatic password generator to help the user with password creation.

The more constraints your security policy puts on creating an adequate password, the more trouble users will have in creating passwords. This may lead to frustration and complaints. To help the user in choosing a password, some account management programs have an automatic password generator that will produce a password according to your security policy criteria. The drawback to using a password generator is that it can create cryptic passwords that may be difficult to remember. Enabling this option, however, will at least provide some help to frustrated users. *Emphasis should be put on choosing your own creative passwords that you can more readily remember.*

INFOSEC Best Practice #80

The password file must be encrypted by the operating system.

Passwords are encrypted by most operating systems. If you are using an old version of an operating system that does not encrypt passwords, upgrade to a newer version of the operating system or modify the login procedure to run your own program which reads a file encrypted by your own method. Storing passwords in a file on your system that is readable by everyone gives you no security and WILL lead to unauthorized access to your system(s). The password file should be modified only by the system administrator.

 INFOSEC Best Practice #81

Restrict access by time of day for high-risk users.

Some users such as part-time employees, temps and consultants may need to be given restricted access to a system only during business hours because they may be considered to be more risky employees. Most operating systems allow the system administrator to set time restrictions on an account based on time of day.

 INFOSEC Best Practice #82

Audit all login attempts and set alarms for repeated incorrect logins.

Keep security logging turned on and check the security log daily. The log will be able to tell the system administrator what is happening on the system and network. Suspicious activity may require more detailed monitoring with a sniffer, increased security protections, and notification of users. This may prevent or diminish the extent of damage if there is an attack on your system.

✓ INFOSEC Best Practice #83

Encrypt passwords that are transmitted over a network.

Authentication of users over a network typically involves sending a password to a file server in clear-text. Therefore, the password is detectable by any sniffer monitoring the network. When choosing an operating system be aware of this problem. Depending on your security policy, you may have to provide third-party mechanisms that encrypt passwords during authentication (e.g., Kerberos authentication, RSA MD4).

✓ INFOSEC Best Practice #84

Create an alternate administrator or system account; do not use the default.

The system account is one of the accounts that is typically attacked by a hacker. Disabling interactive access to it and using another account as the administration account will force the hacker to find another legitimate username. Do not delete the system account since it may be needed by various system functions. Finding a legitimate username may not be difficult because most companies use very similar username naming conventions (e.g., gsmith – first letter of first name followed by last name, smithg – last name followed by first initial, etc.). Other accounts such as the guest account should be disabled and substituted with a less obvious account name. Other default accounts that should be disabled and substituted with new site specific accounts are field maintenance, testing, and database administration.

✓ INFOSEC Best Practice #85

Do not permit users to log on locally to a server.

If users other than an administrator have physical access to a server, then there are a number of things that they can do to try to break into the machine. Keep servers physically secure and do not permit local logon of users other than the system administrator. Some systems differentiate a local account database and network account database. Users should be authenticated onto the network using a network accounts database, not a local accounts database.

✓ INFOSEC Best Practice #86

Use a password to access BIOS setup.

To prevent users from getting around some of your security by booting an operating system from floppy disk, disable booting from floppy in BIOS and password protect your BIOS if your computer allows.

✓ INFOSEC Best Practice #87

Use a screen saver with a password.

When stepping away from your desk for a short period of time use a screen saver that kicks in after a few minutes of idle time and locks your computer with a password. This will prevent users from browsing your computer when it is unattended.

✓ INFOSEC Best Practice #88

Log off the computer when you are finished using it.

In order for your operating system security to have effect, log off your computer when you are done using it at the end of the day or if you will be away from your desk for a longer period of time.

✓ INFOSEC Best Practice #89

Do not keep copies of passwords for system access or decryption on the same machine that uses the password.

It is a good practice not to keep password lists on computers, but if it is necessary, then the password(s) must not be kept on the same machine that uses the password for access or decryption. Hackers look for files containing passwords that can gain them access to other machines, so don't make it easy for them.

9.4 FILE SYSTEM PROTECTION

File system protection is the next logical step in securing an operating system for use by multiple users. This is considered to be one of the key security requirements for C2 security. A poorly protected file system allows hackers or unscrupulous employees to gain access to files and data that may contain sensitive information.

✓ INFOSEC Best Practice #90

System administrators must have full access to all files.

Since system administrators are called upon to help users with a variety of problems, they must be able to get at user files. This makes it important that system administrators be chosen carefully for their trustworthiness. Often system administrators are chosen strictly for their academic and experience qualifications, but they should also be evaluated on their background in terms of trustworthiness. The system administrator can be the biggest security threat to the organization if not chosen wisely. Perform background checks on system administrators.

✔ **INFOSEC Best Practice #91**

Limit remote server administration to the system administrator.

Remote administration of servers is becoming a necessity in many organizations given the proliferation of servers and the reduction in information systems staff. Often, system administrators are required to administer more than one system for many departments within the organization. Remote administration allows the system manager to manage remote systems that are spread out throughout the organization without being physically present. Remote administration helps the system administrator be more efficient at the job and to solve problems quicker. Also, if there are local pseudo-system administrators that take care of the day-to-day tasks, then they may inadvertently have access to more machines within a domain than desirable. Often for convenience reasons, security is relaxed and the system administrator divulges the password for remote administration of some of the machines either by pressure from departments or just for convenience. Under this pressure the system administrator may divulge the password to solve a near-term problem, but in turn opens up a long-term security hole. To maintain security and not cave into the near-term pressures of any department, you must refer back to the official corporate security policy approved by the administration.

✔ **INFOSEC Best Practice #92**

Perform server administration at the console.

If system administration activities are taking place at the system administrator's office, then people can walk into the office and potentially see passwords, file protections, sensitive data, etc. Also, the system administrator may leave momentarily without securing the computer and thereby allow privileged access to the system. Therefore, system administration activities should preferably be done in a restricted area.

✔ INFOSEC Best Practice #93

Set file access rights for groups of users.

All files must be accessed using group access rights. Individual users must belong to groups. Groups can be organized in a hierarchical group structure. Files must not have rights associated for individual users since it is difficult to track, clean-up and change files distributed throughout the system. If a user should not access a file, then that user's account should be transferred to a more restrictive group. Cleaning up file protections becomes much easier.

✔ INFOSEC Best Practice #94

Restrict network file access by network share permissions that are granted on a need to use basis only.

Files accessed via a network connection on virtual drives must have network file access permissions. This is another layer of security on top of file protection. Network access of files on a virtual drive must be group controlled. Both network share permissions and individual file permissions are used to restrict access to a file. This multi-level access control is very important because there are many users on an organization's entire network, including the internet, that may have access to virtual file services. Virtual file services on single user operating systems such as MS Windows 98 should be protected with passwords. An example of virtual file services are NFS (Network File System) a UNIX based system which has also been ported to Microsoft NT and 95, and Microsoft NT's network shares using SMB (System Message Block) communication.

 ### INFOSEC Best Practice #95

Set default file protection to be as restrictive as possible.

When installing a new operating system, the system administrator must first protect the entire file system for his own access only, and then incrementally open directories and files to those users with a need to access. Some operating systems have default protections open to everyone. The system administrator should not rely on defaults, but secure the system according to his or her own file protection best practices. Set file permissions for system administrators to full access (i.e., Read, Write, Execute, Delete, Change Ownership, etc.), but selectively restrict access for users based on their type of access needs. If a user only needs to execute a file, then give the group that the user belongs to "Execute" permission only. If a user should have the option of editing a file, provide "Write" access. Any combination of permissions may be given, but should be as restrictive as possible.

INFOSEC Best Practice #96

Prevent users from viewing all directory names down a
directory tree.

All directory names in a directory tree should not be seen by those
users that do not have a need to access files at that directory level. The
user should not have the option of exploring directories throughout the
system in order to get clues to the type of information that is stored
within those directories. Therefore, set permissions on directories so
that users can have access down a directory tree without seeing the
name of unauthorized directories. For instance, the higher up the directory hierarchy a user goes, the closer the user is to system related
directories.

INFOSEC Best Practice #97

Use access control lists to restrict access to files by
individual users.

To further restrict access to files by a specific user, use access control
lists to specify the type of access a user can have for a particular file.
Even though a user may belong to a group that has full access to a file, an
access control list can restrict a user specifically. When a user attempts to
access a file, the operating system checks the user's access tokens to
determine if any further restrictions found in the list should apply.

INFOSEC Best Practice #98

Clean the swap or page file before releasing a computer to another party.

If a computer is reassigned to another user and it had originally stored sensitive data, then clean the swap or page file on the system. The swap or page file may still contain sensitive data that was paged out of physical memory to the pagefile on disk. There are software programs available that clean these swap or page files.

 INFOSEC Best Practice #99

Do not install more than one operating system on your computer.

If a less secure operating system is installed on your computer, then access can be granted by booting the less secure operating system. Also, do not have multiple versions of the same operating system for the same reason. Usually, the most current operating system is the most secure. This does not apply for developers working on projects requiring multiple operating systems.

9.5 VIRUS PROTECTION

 INFOSEC Best Practice #100

Use a virus scanner on every computer.

There are approximately 100 new viruses created every month. If you exchange files with other users or are connected to the internet, then you are susceptible to viruses. Even software officially distributed by vendors has been known to contain viruses. Since viruses can immobilize your computer and your productivity, destroy files on your system, and even damage the hardware on your system; it is imperative that virus protection be deployed on every computer. Viruses often create unusual, hard to duplicate symptoms that are different to diagnose. The user often does NOT guess that the cause may be a virus because the symptoms appear as if there may be a bug in the program or that the user is doing something wrong. Countless hours are lost trying to fix the problem or work around it. The best protection is to immunize the system with a virus scanner.

Each server must have virus-scanning software that scans any files from external sources. Anti-virus software must scan all incoming IP traffic from the internet, including incoming email and have support to scan some of the more common word processing files and macros. Also, if the server is used to backup any remote machines, the backup software should have a built in anti-virus scanner to scan files before being backed up. A backup report should note if viruses were found.

✔ INFOSEC Best Practice #101

Perform virus scanning of all IP packets at the bastion hosts and the gateway.

Scan all IP traffic coming into the site for viruses before it is sent to any machine on the internal network. Scanners should pick up most viruses if their databases are maintained on a monthly basis. Macro viruses embedded in word processing or spreadsheets must have virus scanners that can detect these types of viruses.

 INFOSEC Best Practice #102

> Download the latest virus signatures for your virus scanner software every two weeks.

Since there are so many new viruses that are created each month, anti-virus software may become obsolete in a relatively short period of time. When you purchase anti-virus software you are usually entitled to download copies of the newest virus databases from the vendor's internet site. The vendors usually update their virus databases a couple of times per month. It is recommended that the user copy the software from the vendor's internet site to make the anti-virus software current and effective against the newest viruses. Most virus scanners have the capability of automatically downloading updates and virus signatures on a set schedule. System administrators and users often forget this task, therefore an automated download method should be used. Alternatively, it is recommended that the system administrator maintain the latest virus signatures on a server and that users have their PCs configured to directly access these files. The system administrator can also push these files down to user PCs. Do *not* get secondhand copies of the anti-virus databases; use the databases from the vendor directly.

INFOSEC Best Practice #103

Perform virus scanning of each machine on a designated schedule.

Install the anti-virus software so that it starts when the system boots and is resident in memory when the system is running. This will provide continuous monitoring for viruses that may arrive at the computer either via floppy disks, mail, or the internet. A virus scanner will not guarantee a virus-free computer, but will significantly reduce the chance of a virus being present. Occasionally, some programs are incompatible with the anti-virus software. If this is the case, you must run your anti-virus software manually on a regular schedule once a week. Servers must be running anti-virus software continuously.

9.6 NETWORK FILE SHARING SECURITY

Most network file systems have some type of security weakness. The administrator must be aware of these problems and decide between the convenience of having network file services and the security holes that may be open when these services are used.

 INFOSEC Best Practice #104

Do not have virtual file services enabled for bastion host machines.

Virtual file services can be a method of accessing multiple machines once a single machine is compromised. Especially, do not have file services across your firewall. The firewall will need to have a port(s) open for that service and thereby provide a hole for entry into your internal network.

 INFOSEC Best Practice #105

Deploy NFS on an internal network, separated from a public network via a firewall.

If you need to use *NFS* (Network File System), then it must be deployed on an internal network because it uses simple clear-text authentication (e.g., host name user ID and group ID). This may be barely acceptable in secure networks where there is limited access to the network, but is not secure on public networks. UNIX systems will typically use this network file system to share files between users and to set up virtual drives for users. If NFS is to be used in an organization, then it should at a minimum be deployed behind a firewall separating the internal network from an external, public network. To increase security when using NFS, but with a performance decrease, use Secure NFS which uses Secure RPC and AUTH_DES encryption.

 INFOSEC Best Practice #106

Do not use X-Windows for mission-critical applications over a public network.

X-Windows cookies are transmitted over the network in clear text. Therefore, applications with sensitive data must not use X-Windows for network-based windowing on a public network.

9.7 NETWORK SOFTWARE

 **INFOSEC Best Practice #107**

Strictly control IP assignment.

One of the key pieces of information for a hacker is knowledge of the IP address ranges within an organization. Additionally, knowledge of the exact IP address of servers and other mission-critical machines can help a hacker focus an attack on these systems. IP addresses can be obtained by buying a block of addresses from Internic or from an organization's Internet Service Provider. Addresses can be bought as class C licenses (256 addresses) or class B licenses (32,000 addresses). Class B licenses are usually reserved for service providers and large companies. There are very few class B licenses around and they are very expensive. Almost all companies will purchase Class C licenses as blocks of 256. If there is no connection to a public network using IP and there are no plans to hook into such a public network in the future (highly unlikely), then the company can use their own IP addresses when setting up systems. Also, if firewalls and proxy servers are used to separate the internal network from the public network, then all the systems internal to the company do not need legal IP addresses since the proxy server will use its own address to communicate with the public network. Most companies buy blocks of legal licenses because they do not know how they might want to communicate in the future and therefore do not want to have to reconfigure their computers with new IP addresses. You must have legal IPs if you have any machine connected to a public network. Home PCs and small offices will get their IPs through their service provider.

 INFOSEC Best Practice #108

Use host to host authentication between two logical networks.

Operating systems currently do not use security protocols to establish host to host links to mail servers or file servers. By not having authentication software that can determine whether the host you are connecting to is really who it claims to be, the user is vulnerable to an attacker that is mimicking the destination host. Kerberos V5 should be used between two hosts that need to communicate for server based applications. Kerberos 5 is a server-based authentication mechanism that: 1) receives a message containing a user's username and current time encrypted with the user's password, 2) looks up the username to determine the password and, 3) tries to decrypt the encrypted time that was sent. If the Kerberos server can decrypt the current time, then it creates a ticket granting ticket containing a session key and ticket for the Kerberos Ticket Granting Service, encrypts it with your password and sends it to you. In this way the user's password is never transmitted across the network and public key cryptography is not used.

✔ **INFOSEC Best Practice #109**

Start up processes only for desired TCP applications.

Each process (daemon) that is running, but is not used is a potential vulnerability to the system. TCP/IP services such as FTP, Telnet, and others use TCP ports to communicate over the IP network. Potential hackers can try to access these ports and exploit the vulnerabilities of these TCP programs. Also, custom applications and database applications use specific TCP ports for client-server applications. These custom written programs may be more vulnerable than hardened TCP applications and provide a potential point for break-in to the machine. If these programs are running from an administrative account, then the hacker may have full access to the machine. To reduce the risk of potential break-ins through TCP ports, only run those TCP applications that you must use on the machine.

9.8 SECURITY LOGS

✔ **INFOSEC Best Practice #110**

Keep a security event log on your computer.

A security logger should be available as part of the operating system or as a third party product. All servers and workstations with restricted access must run a security logger. The security log must be turned on and record the following categories of events:

1. Logins and logoffs.

2. Object access (logging this data may lead to very large log files).

3. File permission changes.

4. File ownership changes.

5. Security policy changes.

6. Changes in user rights.

7. Group changes for an account.

8. System restarts and shutdowns.

9. Virus scans.

Security logs can grow to take up much disk space therefore the server must have a large enough disk. Periodic maintenance will need to be performed to archive or discard the logs.

✓ INFOSEC Best Practice #111

Review the security log on each server on a daily schedule.

Recording security events is a waste of resources if the system administrator does not review the logs on a daily basis. All it takes is five minutes each day to invoke the security log viewer and scan through the recorded events. Since most machines will have little hacker or mischievous activity, system administrators get complacent and stop reviewing the security log. If the machine is important enough for you to decide that security logging must be turned on in order to comply with your established security policy, then the administrator must treat this task seriously. To ease the tedious nature of this task, there are security monitors available for some operating systems that review the security log automatically according to your designated criteria and issue an alarm about potential security breaches. There is a cost involved in purchasing such software, but it may help in enforcing the security policy at your organization.

 ### INFOSEC Best Practice #112

Archive all security logs.

Security logs should be archived on a periodic basis (i.e., yearly). Keeping archives will allow you to go back and check for suspicious activity (e.g., file and object accesses) that occurs on the system over time.

 ### INFOSEC Best Practice #113

Record security events on your firewall.

Your firewall computers must have security logging turned on. Firewall software has its own security and network event logging which must be turned on in addition to operating system security logging.

PC Operating System Security Rules

Workstation and PC operating systems have a fraction of the features of server operating systems. PCs typically are used by a single person and are shut off at the end of the day. These systems, however, often have a network connection, internet access, email, and can hold personal and corporate data.

This section offers a few best-practice guidelines for use with networks containing PCs and workstations.

✓ **INFOSEC Best Practice #114**

For operating systems with no logon authentication, limit access to the PC by using the "power-on" password option at boot-up.

If using an operating system with few security features (e.g., Microsoft Windows 95), then use a power-on password. The hardware configured password option will require the user to enter a password before the system continues to boot the operating system. Most new PCs have this option. It should be used in locations that are considered not secure. Laptops must have this option enabled. Users must turn their PCs off in order for this option to be used; therefore, it should be integrated as part of your site's security policy. Workstations running UNIX, NT, and OS2 have logon authentication via username and passwords and will not require this option to be turned on.

✓ **INFOSEC Best Practice #115**

Authenticate users by a username and password for access to a computer network.

In PC-based operating systems such as Windows 95 and 98, a username and password is used to log the user into a server domain or network. Use a legitimate password even though the intruder can bypass this option by pressing the CANCEL button. By bypassing using the CANCEL button, the intruder will not be able to access any network drives. Microsoft NT and UNIX systems will require logon authentication that will allow access to network resources.

✓ **INFOSEC Best Practice #116**

Password-protect access to shared drives on a desktop PC.

PCs on the network can share their data with other PCs on the net-work. If files need to be shared between users in a workgroup, then you may need to set up your PC operating system to share your drive. This will open up your PC hard disk to others. In order to limit access to this shared drive, password protect it.

Internet Security Rules

The greatest threat to an organization's network is from a public network such as the internet. A firewall is the first step in isolating the internal network from the internet, as discussed in Section 2. This section discusses email, FTP, TELNET, browser, and NEWS security.

11.1 INTERNET MAIL SECURITY

Electronic mail (email) is used widely by corporations, government, educational institutions, and individuals. Everyone would like their email message to be confidential (private), to arrive as it was sent (have integrity), to be sent to who you think you are sending it to (authenticated), and to be signed by the sender to identify the actual sender (digital signature). To remain compatible with the outside world, however, you must use the email packages that inter-operate with one another. These email packages typically do not incorporate most of these security considerations. An organization or an individual can increase security for some email communications by incorporating the following email best practices.

INFOSEC Best Practice #117

Run the newest versions of mail server software.

If operating your own mail server, use the latest versions of mail server software that may include new security features and fix current problems. By running up-to-date versions of your mail server software, you will enhance your mail security.

 INFOSEC Best Practice #118

Scan all incoming email at the mail server.

Anti-virus software must be setup at the mail server to scan all incoming email traffic for viruses. This is the first level of anti-virus defense that attempts to stop virus-infected traffic before it is disseminated to the PC. Some scanners will scan attachments as well as email content. Anti-virus scanners are not very effective at scanning email that is encoded with encrypted information or word processor, spreadsheet, and graphics documents. Setting up a server-based anti-virus scanner, however, is an important first step in filtering out viruses that may come from the internet world.

✔ **INFOSEC Best Practice #119**

To send mail between servers with enhanced security, use authentication between mail servers.

To be compatible in the internet world, you must be able to talk between mail servers using SMTP (Simple Mail Transport Protocol). SMTP, however, does not offer any sophisticated authentication between servers and therefore is susceptible to attack. Also, SMTP communicates in clear text. Since it is the de facto standard for communication between email servers, it is also receiving the most attention in terms of security improvements. Vendors are beginning to add on features to increase security in their email server offerings. Corporate users that want authentication between their email servers either have to incorporate an authentication scheme on their servers such as Kerberos or implement another email package that includes that feature. Implementing authentication will, however, restrict the interchange of mail between servers that support the authentication that is used. This will most likely limit mail interchange over the internet to mail servers located at different corporate locations.

✔ INFOSEC Best Practice #120

Use password authentication for individual mail accounts.

Mail server software is set up to send mail between servers, receive mail from clients, and send mail to clients. All email accounts within an organization will be set up on a mail server and will require a username to identify individual mail accounts. Each user will have client mail software (e.g., Eudora, Microsoft Outlook) which will be configured to access the user's server-based mail account. In order to access mail, a password must be provided to access the server. That password must follow INFOSEC Best Practices for password selection. It should be a different password from your other passwords because it is usually stored locally at the client PC and may be stored in clear-text.

✓ INFOSEC Best Practice #121

Use email encryption for sending confidential data between two mutually agreed upon clients.

Currently, email is transmitted in plain text across the internet and can be read by any packet sniffing device. If the email is very confidential or has corporate sensitive information, it will need to be encrypted to ensure privacy. The encryption software that is used must be the same at both ends in order for decryption to take place successfully. Mail client software packages such as Eudora and others are beginning to include encryption in their products. Also, there are vendors that sell add-on encryption packages that integrate with existing mail clients. Examples of mail encryption software are S-MIME (Secure MIME), PGP (Pretty Good Privacy), RSA, Diffie-Hellman, and PEM (Privacy Enhanced Mail). PGP is very popular and S-MIME is gaining popularity. Which package wins out as a de facto standard is yet to be determined. For mail encryption to become standard for all email so that it can be sent encrypted to anyone on the internet will require the emergence of a standard. The problem is complicated by the fact that the internet extends across national boundaries, but encryption does not. Anything above standard DES 56-bit encryption is not exportable by US companies. However, packages may be able to support multiple encryption methods for communication among various international sites. Other compatibility problems arise if older encryption packages are used. For instance, an old version of PGP, several revisions out of date, may not be able to communicate with a new version of PGP. Keeping your encryption software up to date becomes important in order to maintain compatibility.

Also, some corporations may want stronger encryption than that offered by any de facto standard. Alternately, rather than the client encrypting mail, extended SMTP servers (ESMTP) can be used to encrypt traffic between two ESMTP servers.

✓ INFOSEC Best Practice #122

For email messages where the identity of the sender needs to be confidential, use an anonymous remailer to send mail with all traces of your identity and internet location removed from the message headers.

For some applications such as sending general mail to a large group of users or to a destination anonymously, use an anonymous emailer. Your actual email address will be protected and will not be available to the internet community. All that will be known is the anonymous mailer's account.

✓ INFOSEC Best Practice #123

Do not have email agents installed on machines for mission-critical operations.

Some email messages may not be passive, but involve active computation by the object enclosed in the message body that can be activated to do damage on a machine (i.e., embedded in postscript files). Leave email programs off of mission-critical machines in order not to be susceptible to attack via email.

 INFOSEC Best Practice #124

> To stop mailings from a known source, send mail to the source with instructions to remove you from their mail list.

Most news groups and other sources that automatically send mail to a list of addresses will have instructions embedded in the mail message on how to unsubscribe. To unsubscribe, send a one-line message to the sender with the appropriate command to unsubscribe (i.e., "UNSUBSCRIBE"). If you do not know how to unsubscribe, then send the webmaster at that site (i.e., webmaster@site.com) a mail message with a request to remove you from the mail list or to send instructions on how to unsubscribe.

✔ **INFOSEC Best Practice #125**

> To protect the mail server against spamming attacks, filter out all consecutive mail messages of the same size using an anti-spamming software package.

Some spam attacks send hundreds or thousands of files to the mail server that overwhelm the mail server software or bog down the processor. These messages tend to be of the same size; therefore they can be recognized by automated software. Anti-spamming software is available from several vendors.

 INFOSEC Best Practice #126

> Use a separate email name when posting your email address to public forums such as news groups and chat sites.

By using a different email name for public forums such as news groups, user groups or chat sites, the name can be easily deleted in order to stop unwanted mail. Posting your original email name may require changing it in the future either by your service provider or by the system administrator at your organization.

11.2 FTP SECURITY

FTP servers are used to retrieve files posted on the server or place files to the server. Publicly accessible FTP servers need to have strong security implemented since users can actually log on to the machine.

✓ **INFOSEC Best Practice #127**

> Install anti-virus software on the FTP server.

Anti-virus software must be installed on each FTP server. All FTP downloads must be scanned before copying the files from the FTP server to an internal PC or server. Anti-virus software is available which will scan all incoming IP traffic to the server.

✔ INFOSEC Best Practice #128

Disable the FTP service on systems not using FTP.

Disable the FTP service on servers that are not designated as FTP servers. Keeping the service enabled allows hackers to log into the machine and check for weaknesses in file system permissions, look for network information, and try to break into the system.

✔ INFOSEC Best Practice #129

For environments where users request specific files by name, set up FTP with a mail interface so that requests for files can be made by mailing a specially formatted request to an alias account.

For environments where users request files, logins to the FTP server can be disabled. A mail interface can be set up to an alias account. The program behind the alias parses the request and mails the requested files in response. Therefore, unknown users do not need to log onto the machine and copy files. Preventing users from actually logging into the FTP server will significantly increase security since the hacker must now find a different entry point. FTP servers are unique in that they allow the general public, including hackers, to actually log into the machines in order to get files.

✓ INFOSEC Best Practice #130

Disable the FTP anonymous and guest accounts.

To distribute files between known individuals or sites, disable anonymous and default guest accounts and set up separate accounts that have a different username and password. These accounts can then be distributed to authenticated users. Several sets of usernames and passwords for different sites or groups of individuals can be used. All users, especially hackers, know that FTP servers often have an anonymous account with no password. Hackers may try to exploit the system via this account.

✓ INFOSEC Best Practice #131

Set permissions on FTP directories for authorized users only.

Set permissions for directories on the FTP server to be closed to public access except those in the FTP directory tree. Permissions must only be accessed by the specific group to which the user belongs.

✓ INFOSEC Best Practice #132

Create a separate disk partition for FTP directories.

A separate disk partition must be created for FTP access. This partition must not contain any system files, applications or system data, but only FTP data. Alternately, disk quotas can be set up to control the amount of disk space available to FTP accounts. Setting up disk partitions or disk quotas will protect the FTP server from denial of service attacks that try to fill up the disk with files.

11.3 TELNET SECURITY

 INFOSEC Best Practice #133

Use a TELNET proxy server for outbound TELNET sessions.

Use a TELNET proxy server for TELNET sessions originating from the internal network. The TELNET proxy server is a highly secure machine that acts as an intermediary between the destination host and the user. The proxy server completes the connection by logging into an account on the destination server and forwards user commands to that machine. It therefore hides internal machine IP addresses and does not allow outbound sessions direct access or unlimited command and connection capability with the destination machine. Public inbound sessions to the internal network must not be allowed. Public machines that need TELNET access must be located on the DMZ.

 INFOSEC Best Practice #134

Disable TELNET on all machines that do not use the service.

Disable the TELNET service on all machines that do not use it. This will prevent hackers from using these ports to try to gain access if your network is compromised. If there are many machines on your network, disabling TELNET on each machine may take too much time. Disable TELNET sessions through the firewall except for authorized machines.

✔ INFOSEC Best Practice #135

For data sensitive applications, use a Kerberized TELNET.

A Kerberized TELNET will require authentication between the originating and destination machines and will encrypt the session. This will require Kerberos to be configured on both machines where TELNET communication will take place. It is meant for specific applications and not general internet use.

11.4 BROWSER SECURITY

✔ INFOSEC Best Practice #136

Do not allow browsers on mission-critical machines.

Since browsers download data from external web servers for interpretation by the browser, the computer will be vulnerable to viruses, IP divulgence, and malicious programs. If these machines are running mission-critical systems, then do not deploy a browser. Some system managers may think of this as an inconvenience, but it will reduce the security risk on that machine and should be addressed in the security policy.

✔ **INFOSEC Best Practice #137**

Use browsers that support the SSL or SHHTP protocols for secure internet communication.

In e-commerce applications, the transfer of credit card numbers will require that the browser support SSL (Secure Sockets Layer) or SHTTP. The SET protocol for commerce credit card transactions is an example of a protocol that requires SSL. Any application that requires privacy will have to have some form of encryption and a secure end-to-end connection established. SSL is a system that provides an encrypted TCP/IP connection between two computers on the Internet. It can be used to encrypt any TCP/IP protocol such as FTP, TELNET, and HTTP using public-key encryption. The server that will support SSL will need to have a server id issued by a certificate authority. Alternatively, SHTTP is a system developed by Netscape that is different from SSL and only encrypts HTTP.

✔ **INFOSEC Best Practice #138**

Use browsers that support 128-bit encryption.

Some government and industrial e-commerce web sites require that the browser support 128-bit encryption in order to communicate. 128-bit encryption greatly decreases the chance that data will be deciphered. Most browsers support the standard 56-bit encryption, but data can be deciphered using high-power computers. The restriction for 128-bit browsers is that distribution is limited within the US; it cannot be exported. If performing encrypted web access internationally, then it will be necessary to use 56-bit encryption.

✓ INFOSEC Best Practice #139

Use an application gateway that proxies HTTP sessions in order to hide the identity of internal machines.

For users on an internal network that need to keep their computer IP address and identity private, yet need to communicate with the internet, use an application gateway that proxies HTTP sessions.

✓ INFOSEC Best Practice #140

Secure the server from the directory root downward with SSL.

By securing your system with SSL from the root down, data transfer to or from the server will be secure. If the server is not secured from the root down, then a hacker can copy files to an unsecured directory. Also, someone can accidentally place sensitive data in an unsecure directory that can be accessed with standard HTTP.

✓ INFOSEC Best Practice #141

Execute Java applets within your browser.

Do not download and execute Java applets and programs outside the browser environment. Browsers include Java security that by default considers all applets as untrusted and thereby does not allow access to local system information. The Java virtual machine and Java security model look for Java applet security problems. Stronger client-side protection against Java applets can be handled by software at the firewall (that can be purchased off-the-shelf) to inspect Java content as it enters your network.

 INFOSEC Best Practice #142

Block ActiveX modules at the firewall.

It is highly recommended that ActiveX modules be selectively blocked or entirely blocked at the firewall. ActiveX must be blocked from unknown sources because the module may contain malicious code. ActiveX modules are more dangerous than Java applets since they have access to the desktop and can call any system process. The security model in Microsoft Explorer warns against unsigned ActiveX modules, but that is not a very good safeguard. Alternatively, software can be acquired that inspects and filters HTTP traffic for applets, ActiveX components, JavaScript, VBScript, ZIP files, and others. This type of product is installed on the server and can scan HTTP traffic if it is required to have access to ActiveX and Java applets.

11.5 NEWS SECURITY

 INFOSEC Best Practice #143

Set up disk quotas or create a separate disk partition on the NNTP server.

If you subscribe to internet NEWS, then your NNTP (Network News Transport Protocol) server may be attacked via excessive NEWS delivery that may fill up your disk and/or use up your internet bandwidth for an unacceptably long period of time. NEWS requires very large amounts of disk space that may reach a gigabyte or more each week. NNTP software is available which only downloads those newsgroups that have active local members and not the entire distribution. This should limit the amount of disk space and bandwidth needed to accomplish the task over an internet connection. If the internet connection is slow, then it may not be possible to do this type of activity at all. Setting up disk quotas or creating a separate disk partition for news will prevent NEWS updates or hacker distributed data from filling the disk.

SECTION 12

Application Security Rules

Use the guidelines in this section to enhance security at the application software level.

✔ INFOSEC Best Practice #144

All applications that are highly confidential must have application-level authentication of the user.

To gain access to an application that uses or displays highly confidential or sensitive data, an application level of user authentication must be used. When a confidential application is launched it must authenticate the user via a password or device such as a smart card. Data stored by this application must be encrypted. If an unauthorized person or hacker breaks into the system, you will have an additional layer of protection for your sensitive data.

INFOSEC Best Practice #145

Encrypt all data in sensitive client-server applications.

For applications that are accessing or transferring sensitive data using a client-server application over a corporate network, encryption of the data will ensure data confidentiality. The type of encryption that must be used depends on the level of sensitivity of the data. Data can be encrypted by software prior to transmission or by hardware that encrypts all IP traffic between compatibly configured sites.

 INFOSEC Best Practice #146

Create separate accounts to run web and application processes.

Hackers will have a more difficult time modifying the processes that have to be run out of secure accounts if they break into one of the standard user accounts on the system.

Software Validation and Verification Rules

Evaluating all software installed on an organization's computers can be a major security plus, if done correctly. This section offers several basic rules for validating and verifying software.

✓ INFOSEC Best Practice #147

Perform a security validation and verification procedure on all mission-critical custom software to be deployed on the network.

For mission-critical custom applications, perform application security validation and verification (V&V). Check for back doors, error handling, illegal termination, system function calls, kernel mode operations, access control, malicious code and monitoring code (used for eavesdropping and condition checking in order to activate malicious code). This is a costly process that is done beyond regular V&V and must be done for those applications that will be processing very sensitive data.

✔ **INFOSEC Best Practice #148**

Remove all source code, compilers and linkers from mission-critical systems.

By removing all source code, compilers, and linkers from the system on which the application is running, a hacker will not be able to make modifications to the application.

✔ **INFOSEC Best Practice #149**

Vendor supplied Commercial-Off-The-Shelf software must be evaluated for its impact on the security of mission-critical systems.

In larger organizations it is cost effective to do this once for a product and share the information with the community of potential users. This evaluation would involve hands-on testing of the product from a security perspective. Smaller companies, however, are forced to use third-party evaluations from testing labs or technical publications not affiliated with any of the vendors.

✔ **INFOSEC Best Practice #150**

Evaluate software developed by a consulting firm for security vulnerabilities.

When you receive custom software developed for your organization by a consulting firm, evaluate the software before deploying it on your mission-critical systems. Hackers working for software companies may build in a backdoor to the system during development. Even though this is rare, check out your custom, mission-critical software before deployment.

 INFOSEC Best Practice #151

> On mission-critical systems, scan all new distribution media for viruses.

All new software distributions must be scanned by the vendor for viruses. There have been incidents, although rare, where vendors have distributed software or newly formatted floppies with viruses on the disk(s). Also, scan new media before writing onto it.

 INFOSEC Best Practice #152

> Check for illegal software on a routine schedule on all mission-critical systems.

Unauthorized programs on mission-critical systems may not have been checked for their security impact. These programs may come from a dubious source, may be infected with a virus or create a back door for entry into the system. The programs may violate your security policy and therefore make your mission-critical systems more vulnerable. Publicly available software that resides on a system provides an opportunity for a hacker to exploit weaknesses in the software.

INFOSEC Best Practice #153

All software must be received from an official and legal source.

Do not install software from home or from privately acquired or unknown sources. If the origin of a software package is unknown, do not install it. Software programs may have malicious code that can destroy your system or open up a back door into your system. Data that is obtained from an unknown source or whose original source is unknown should be scanned first for viruses.

 INFOSEC Best Practice #154

Perform checksum verification of software that has been transferred across a public communication channel.

Files sent across the internet can be intercepted and modified. Perform a checksum on mission-critical files when transmitted across a public access communication channel such as the internet. Perform a checksum on custom software deployed on multiple systems to ensure that you are using the same software from a configuration management point of view and that it has not been corrupted or changed in any way during the transfer process from one system to the next. Also, critical operating system files and application programs must be checked to ensure that these files were not modified by unauthorized persons. Hackers sometimes substitute their own system programs with the same name to create a back door that provides monitoring capability of the network. Checksums done on a regular, even automated, basis may catch these problems. Send the checksum separately along a different distribution channel so that it cannot be intercepted and modified.

✔ INFOSEC Best Practice #155

Remove all unnecessary software from servers.

The more software resident on a server, the more chances are provided to the hacker of finding a hole into your system. Remove all sample software and unnecessary source code. Run only the software that is needed on each server. For publicly accessible servers, have each server run a single application only (e.g., mail server, FTP server, web server, etc.).

Data Encryption Rules

Some organizations have a need for encryption of data stored on computers and sent across networks. This section provides a set of guidelines for implementing and managing data encryption.

✔ **INFOSEC Best Practice #156**

> Standardize on the type of encryption used at the organization.

Data can be encrypted either through hardware or software, using various encryption schemes. In order for your organization to exchange encrypted data, all sites will have to agree on the encryption method. Letting every site, group, department, or individual choose their own encryption scheme will result in too much technical management and will limit how the company can communicate between sites and ensure privacy. Multi-level security (MLS) can be specified for various types of communication within an organization. For instance, very confidential financial data will require stronger encryption than email between some employees. These levels of security must be evaluated and incorporated into the organization's security policy. Once the policy specifies the strength of encryption for various levels of data within the corporate framework, then specific encryption software and/or hardware can be chosen. Exceptions will include encryption requirements for communicating externally to other non-corporate sites.

✓ INFOSEC Best Practice #157

Use encryption when transmitting sensitive or confidential data over a network.

Data encryption and decryption can be accomplished by either hardware or software. Data can be encrypted on the computer, stored encrypted in a file, and transmitted over the network using conventional protocols. Encryption is the most straightforward way to keep data confidential on a computer and when transferring the data across a network.

Since applications must use data in unencrypted form, data must be encrypted in a separate step prior to transmission across a network. Software exists which intercepts data between the application and the TCP/IP sockets layer and encrypts the IP packets before they go out onto the IP network. In this case the same software must exist on the receiving machine to decrypt the data that was transmitted. This process is transparent to the user. An alternative to the software encryption of IP packets is to use an encrypting network card or encrypting device between the network and the computer. These hardware devices are faster than software, so they can handle a higher throughput of data.

The military community uses Fortezza adapter cards with encryption that is used to transfer sensitive, but not secret, data. These devices use DES (data encryption standard) encryption. Stronger encryption devices are available through vendors such as Motorola and must be NSA approved. Government classified communication must comply with Federal security guidelines such as the Orange Book, DoD 5200.28-STD "Department of Defense Trusted Computer System Evaluation Criteria," and Green Book "Security of Information Systems." Fortezza Plus (Krypton) cards are designed to be used for Confidential and Secret information that must be transmitted over unclassified networks. These cards require Fortezza adapter drivers that must be supported by the computer's operating system. Unclassified systems that require transmission of sensitive or confidential data can use either software-based encryption or Fortezza cards.

 ## INFOSEC Best Practice #158

Use strong encryption implemented in hardware when transferring secret or financial data between sites.

Implementing a hardware-based strong encryption will guarantee that the data being transmitted across a network from one machine to another will be encrypted. Since the hardware will be attached to the output port of the network adapter on the computer it will be present between your computer and the network. No misconfiguration of your computer software will compromise the encryption. In order for machines with secret or highly confidential data to attach to the network, the organization's security policy must require that this encryption hardware be used at both sending and receiving ends.

✓ **INFOSEC Best Practice #159**

Use at least 128-bit encryption for encrypting sensitive data.

For systems requiring high confidentiality of sensitive data, encrypt data using at least 128-bit encryption such as 128-bit triple DES.

✓ **INFOSEC Best Practice #160**

Encrypt all data corresponding to its level of classification.

The strength of encryption for any piece of data must be determined by your organization's classification of that data. The more private a piece of information, the greater the strength of encryption that is needed. An organization should label its information in a similar way as the government – unclassified, confidential, secret, top secret or use its own complementary designation (i.e., non-sensitive, confidential, sensitive, highly sensitive). Once data classifications are set, then an encryption scheme can be associated with that data. Typically, data of differing security levels should not be resident on the same machine. The government is currently testing multi-level security concepts (MLS) for their military applications where each piece of data has an associated classification label. The operating system must be able to determine who can view data with different labels. Currently, this technology is still too immature and costly to implement, but in the future may be bundled with mainstream operating systems.

✓ INFOSEC Best Practice #161

Store information with different security classifications on separate computers.

Store data with different security classifications on separate computer systems. Only individuals with the authorized level of access will be able to logon to the computer and access the data. Keeping information of differing classification levels on the same computer using conventional operating systems and encryption makes the data vulnerable for access by unauthorized individuals due to misconfiguration of operating system security.

✓ INFOSEC Best Practice #162

Separate computers with sensitive data from computers with lesser classification levels using a firewall.

Computers with financial data, human resource data, and other secret information must be separated from other computers with less sensitive data by a firewall or reside on a separate network. If there is a requirement to make some of the financial data available to a larger population of users, then a firewall will be the most practical solution in that it will allow the transfer of data to publicly accessible machines while maintaining security. Alternatively, data can be put into a data warehouse that is accessible to a larger audience. Data that is extremely sensitive, which may compromise the stability of your organization, must exist on a separate network not connected to any public network.

INFOSEC Best Practice #163

Use server certificates from a recognized "key" distribution center for exchanging corporate sensitive information.

Encryption is not enough to maintain security of private data. In order to ensure that the destination to which data is being sent is really the intended receiving site and not a false site disguised as the destination site, digital certificates are used to identify servers. These certificates allow users to have confidence that the holder of the certificate is who he says he is. Before data is exchanged, certificates are checked. In order to get a certificate from a certificate granting authority, you must generate a private key-pair on your computer. The key-pair has a private key that is used by the entity generating the key to decrypt messages destined for it. No one else possesses this key. Each person or entity, such as a computer, will have their own private key that can open or decrypt files destined for that person or system only. When the key pair is created, it also has a public key that is used by the population to encrypt messages destined to that person or system. The certificate authority publishes your public key so that anyone who wants to send you a private message can encrypt that message with your public key and only you can decrypt it with your private key. The level of trust lies with the certificate authority checking you out and making sure you are who you say you are. Therefore, the person using the public key has confidence that his private message will be delivered to the correct person identified by the public key. A certificate can also be issued to a server to authenticate the server as the machine it identifies itself as.

INFOSEC Best Practice #164

> Use public keys that are certified by the owner or a trusted
> source.

Accept public keys only from trusted sources. It is possible for public keys to be tampered with, such as a hacker posting or substituting a public key with someone else's identification. Therefore, getting keys directly from the source or a trusted source such as an associate, friend or a certificate authority is essential for security.

 INFOSEC Best Practice #165

> Protect your own private key and pass phrase by keeping it
> in a physically secure location that is known only by you.

Keep your own private key in a secure location that is accessible only by you. This can be a locked file drawer with keys that only you possess. If you use a computer at work, keep the private key at some other location. Try not to keep this information on a computer that may be accessed by other people or written down where other people have access.

 INFOSEC Best Practice #166

> Establish a key management policy.

Once keys are created for many people and servers in your organization it will be necessary to have a way of managing the keys. If employees leave, or delete their keys, then the organization must have a way of recovering from that scenario. There must be a centralized key management facility that issues a key-pair to any new server or individual. The key management facility must be backed up by the organization and the data stored in a secure location. Another advantage to a centralized key facility is that public key names can be issued that are consistent and approved by an organization's security policy.

INFOSEC Best Practice #167

Wipe the plain-text versions of encrypted files from the computer hard disk.

After encrypting a file, the remaining plain-text file must be wiped from the disk. The normal operating system "delete" command marks blocks on the disk as deleted so that the space can be reused, but does not erase the actual data on disk. Third party software is available to overwrite (wipe) the deleted plain text file data blocks on disk so that the original data cannot be recovered by unauthorized people. This software can optionally overwrite each of the blocks on disk many times so that these blocks cannot be recovered by sophisticated hardware and techniques that try to detect the faint magnetic traces of the original data.

Configuration Management Rules

This section provides several essential guidelines pertaining to configuring systems on the network.

✓ **INFOSEC Best Practice #168**

Keep track of all files on each computer using an authorized tracking and configuration management program.

You can keep track of all software deployed on a single computer with purchased software-tracking programs. All legal software can be tracked by an organization on each networked computer using a server-based tracking system. Keeping only authorized software on a system will reduce the chance that compromised programs are introduced into the system that can be used to disable individual computers and attack your computer network. An alternative to software tracking programs is to set up your own tracking system where software is checked into a clearing site within your IS organization and logged onto a database.

This philosophy is good only for small organizations with 1-50 computers, but not effective for larger organizations because of the labor involved.

The organization must have a procedure for tracking software since it is the responsibility of each organization to prevent rampant copying of software by employees. Each employee should sign a document from the human resources department agreeing not to copy software. Also, do not allow employees to install software that is brought from home or that is not officially logged into the system. This is becoming a more difficult problem since many vendors are distributing software via the internet which bypasses all corporate tracking procedures. To keep track of all software on a system, software-tracking programs should be purchased and used.

 INFOSEC Best Practice #169

A code management program must be used to track all major software development for custom INFOSEC applications.

Misconfigurations of INFOSEC software can compromise the security of a system and network. A code management program applied to custom code will minimize the chance of misconfiguration of your software. Misconfiguration can com- promise any built-in security in your application. The configuration management program must keep a history of file revisions.

✓ **INFOSEC Best Practice #170**

Frequently review postings on web pages so that the data does not compromise security to your network or reveal sensitive data.

There is so much data being posted on websites that some sensitive information that should be restricted ends up on the internet. This data may include phone numbers to modems on computers that are directly connected to the internal network or data revealing sensitive information that should not be made available to the public.

Network Monitoring Rules

An essential element of a solid INFOSEC system is monitoring hardware/software, used to keep tabs on performance, problems, and security issues. This section offers some basic rules for installing and using monitoring equipment and procedures.

✔ **INFOSEC Best Practice #171**

Install network sniffers and network monitoring software on your network.

Network monitoring equipment must be used to troubleshoot hardware problems, analyze performance, and monitor security as needed. Monitoring the network involves the use of hardware and software to detect the packet type, volume of packets, origin and destination of packets, physical characteristics of the wiring, physical layout of the network, and the presence of devices on the network. These sniffers must be able to do this for each of the protocols on the network. Typically, besides TCP/IP, Microsoft networking uses NetBEUI and Netware uses IPX/SPX. Also, all this activity must be able to be logged by the sniffer.

A network sniffer must be connected to the network to detect a SYN attack by a hacker. Having a sniffer attached to the network will provide an early warning to system administrators about hackers trying to identify your open TCP ports using a SYN program.

Network sniffer software must be deployed on a laptop computer so that it can be taken to the location with a problem. Often, the network is segmented by switches, hubs and routers. Therefore, bringing the monitoring platform to the area experiencing the problem will help diagnose the problem quicker. Sophisticated monitoring and management software that looks at the entire network and talks to network devices throughout the organization can be deployed on a dedicated workstation that graphically displays the layout of portions of your network and the status of its various devices. Typically, since hardware and software is expensive, networks over 100 nodes will need a network sniffer and networks over 500 nodes will need network monitoring and management software.

Network topology must be graphically displayed by segment since larger networks will not be able to be seen in their entirety with all detail. Devices on the network such as routers, switches, hubs, repeaters, PCs, servers, printers and other devices should be represented graphically with the name of the device appearing on the screen. Traffic conditions on each segment should be displayed in color and change dynamically. New nodes that appear on the network should be displayed with a flashing red color, alarm, and log.

The network monitoring software must be able to detect changes to the network, log these changes and invoke alarms based on criteria set by the network manager. Network connections from source to destination and traffic on each logical network segment must be logged. Also, alarms must be logged.

INFOSEC Best Practice #172

Train network managers to use network monitoring
equipment and software.

Network monitoring equipment and software may have many features and be difficult to operate. Without learning the functionality of the monitoring equipment you will not be able to take full advantage of the functionality of the equipment and may increase the time it takes to diagnose your network or INFOSEC problem. Spend time learning the equipment and send the network administrator to a class on the product.

 INFOSEC Best Practice #173

Use network devices that communicate using a site
standardized network management protocol.

In order to use monitoring software on your network that will give you useful information, devices that support a network management protocol such as SNMP must be used. Since most sites will already have established networks and have many devices on the networks, many of these devices will not support SNMP. New purchases must support network management and have features which provide information about the status of the device over the network. Key devices that would affect large portions of the network such as switches and routers may need to be replaced with the highest priority in order to enhance the monitoring of key network components.

INFOSEC Best Practice #174

Archive all logged information on a set schedule.

Since logs get large quickly, old logs should be put on tape or CD and archived in your data repository on a set schedule. Archive logs once a month.

 INFOSEC Best Practice #175

To monitor for unauthorized sniffers on the network, check whether the interfaces on the network are in promiscuous mode.

Hackers will monitor a network using sniffing software that will set network interfaces (e.g., network adapters) to promiscuous mode in order to accept all packets. Programs are available to detect promiscuous mode, as are utilities on many systems. For example, UNIX systems have a command "ifconfig –a" that will return information about all the interfaces and if they are set to promiscuous mode. Hackers often know about these commands and may replace them with their own copy to try to avoid detection. Verify the checksum on these programs before use.

Maintenance and Troubleshooting Security Rules

Once your information security system is in place and operating effectively, the main focus turns to maintenance and troubleshooting, areas which can also lead to security problems. This section addresses the most important rules for handling regular maintenance and for troubleshooting any problems that arise.

✔ INFOSEC Best Practice #176

All users that perform maintenance operations on a computer must keep a written log of activity.

Maintenance that is performed on hardware or software must be written to a log book or computer file. Modifications, patches and updates to the system may open up security holes inadvertently and a logbook may provide a clue to the problem. The biggest problem in keeping a logbook is ensuring that system administrators, network administrators, and computer maintenance personnel actually keep the log current. Keeping a log is a best practice that makes it easier to solve problems.

INFOSEC Best Practice #177

Keep up to date with security information about new vulnerabilities to current operating systems and software.

Security can be increased by installing software patches that update security vulnerabilities. Software vendors post patches on their websites to known security flaws and bugs. Download these patches regularly and keep your system updated. Read all CERT advisories and consider subscribing to security and hacker magazines. See Appendix A for incident response centers, security web sites, and security mailing lists.

 INFOSEC Best Practice #178

Keep up to date with newly released security software that may enhance security.

There is a constant stream of new software packages that are focused on solving some security problem. Keep up to date with new hardware and software that may enhance security. The cost of security products is dropping as more sites acquire security products, making it more reasonable for small as well as large sites to afford these products. For a list of some security related software see (www.sans.org).

✓ **INFOSEC Best Practice #179**

Test mission-critical systems using a security tool.

A software tool or suite of tools that tries to break into your system should be obtained and used on a quarterly basis or after major software changes, patches, reconfigurations and operating system updates. The tool should try to break into TCP ports, and compromise the security of your operating system. Using such a tool will test the effectiveness of your security configuration and policy.

✓ **INFOSEC Best Practice #180**

Run your own attack scenarios against your system.

Run your own attack scenarios against your system to discover weaknesses and vulnerabilities that may not be picked up by a single tool. Plug up as many holes into your system and network as possible and run the scenarios at regular intervals.

✓ **INFOSEC Best Practice #181**

Keep a supply of spare network devices.

Information security problems as well as network problems can be diagnosed more quickly by replacing devices on the network. Most of these devices are inexpensive such as network adapter cards and hubs.

✓ **INFOSEC Best Practice #182**

Require vendors to use smart cards to dial into your system.

Some vendors may need dial-in access to your systems in order to maintain their products. In the process, new software may be downloaded to your system. This can be done via a modem connection to the vendor site. For increased security, host to host authentication must be established, access control should be via a smart card, and the vendor account must be disabled after each session. The vendor must inform you when maintenance is to be done, upon which time the field maintenance account can be enabled for that time period only. The login session by the vendor must be recorded by the system administrator and reviewed. Also, the system must be rescanned for viruses. For mission-critical systems, the organization must decide whether having a vendor link is too high a security risk. This type of link, even though it can be encrypted and have end-to-end authentication, introduces an external connection directly to the mission-critical system that may compromise security. Mission-critical systems may have to trade-off quick problem resolution against reduced security. Use the risk index to determine the tradeoff and decide which mission-critical system should have this vendor maintenance convenience.

 INFOSEC Best Practice #183

Maintain a backup schedule for backing up data on each server.

Backing up data on a daily basis is an essential function of system administration. By using backup tapes, data and the operating system can be restored after a hacker attack or system failure. Full backups must be done weekly, and incremental backups done daily. A sufficient supply of tapes must be available to perform weekly full backups through the archive period. When the data is archived, usually on a quarterly basis, the tapes can start to be rotated for the next archive period. Incremental backups must be rotated weekly. Most enterprise-oriented backup software for servers can perform image backups that record the entire disk bit by bit. If the system has a catastrophic failure, then the image can be dumped onto the fixed system by booting off of a floppy or CD. With the image backup feature, the user does not have to reinstall the operating system, layered products, and data one by one. Instead, the entire system since the last image backup can be dumped onto a newly initialized disk and brought up to date using weekly and incremental backups. An image-save should be done whenever there are any system changes.

 INFOSEC Best Practice #184

Maintain procedures for doing backups, restoring files, and recovering deleted or corrupted data.

If data is corrupted or deleted either intentionally or unintentionally, then there should be a procedure in place to fix the problem. Some operating systems allow you to undelete data from the disk using a third-party utility. If data is deleted and it was not created the same day, then the incremental or full backup will have the data. A written procedure is a good idea in order to restore data when the systems staff is not available. Someone unfamiliar with the backup software can follow the procedure and restore the necessary data. Backup privileges can be assigned to people outside of the normal IT staff to help out in emergencies. One of the problems in most information systems departments is that procedures to do certain tasks are not written down. When there is a problem, and the appropriate personnel are not available, then there is a frantic scramble to figure out how to solve the problem.

✓ INFOSEC Best Practice #185

Place backed-up data in a secure location that is environmentally protected.

Backups of mission-critical data should be kept off-site in a secure facility that is fireproof, waterproof, temperature and humidity controlled, and has strong access control. Backups of organizational data that are not mission critical should be stored in a different building, floor, or room from the computer facility. Each of these locations should have secure access.

✓ INFOSEC Best Practice #186

Archive data at least quarterly.

Archive your data periodically and store it for as long as you need. Archive backups should be separate from your regular backup procedure and be placed in your backup storage facility for as long as you want to keep data. It is a good idea to make archives on at least a quarterly basis during the year.

INFOSEC Best Practice #187

Backup PCs on your network periodically.

If the organization is large and has many PCs, it may be impractical to backup all data on PC disks given a limited network bandwidth. However, if your network bandwidth is adequate, PCs should be backed up at least once a month. For instance, each department in an organization can be backed up on a different day. Alternatively, if bandwidth is limited, configure your servers with network file services where users can store important files. Servers should always be backed up.

 INFOSEC Best Practice #188

Server Emergency Repair Disks should be stored at a secure location.

A copy of these emergency repair disks should be kept locally, but should be only accessible to the system administrator.

Training

Training takes money. Management would rather hire previously trained individuals. Ongoing projects cannot be interrupted for the sake of training. All these are valid points, but do not solve the problem that if people are not trained to address a problem, that problem will not be addressed. In the area of information security, lack of training of system administrators and lack of awareness by users exposes the organization to an increased security risk. The risk can directly translate to loss of revenue due to system or network downtime, data loss and unavailability, and negative impact on corporate image. Since companies often do not take information security seriously, training in information security is taken less seriously. The bottom line is – if you don't train your staff on information security, it will not be implemented effectively nor enforced.

✔ INFOSEC Best Practice #189

Train staff and upper management on the importance of information security to the operation of their organization.

One of the major reasons for poor information security is that most upper management believes that the risk is very low that their systems will be compromised via external attack. System administrators who do believe that INFOSEC solutions need to be implemented and go to management for approval of expenditures are often rejected. The common thought is that if it hasn't happened up until now, it is unlikely to happen in the future and therefore there are more pressing problems to be addressed first.

 INFOSEC Best Practice #190

Train users on Best Practices from a user's perspective.

Users should know how to secure their own PCs either at work or at home and should be aware of data privacy, authentication, and integrity issues. Also, users should be aware of how hackers can attack organizational networks. Emphasis should be placed on password maintenance, methods to check and counter viruses, backups, and mail privacy. New employees should receive some security training during their orientation.

 INFOSEC Best Practice #191

Train network administrators on INFOSEC Best Practices.

The network administrator in most small- to medium-sized organizations acts as the security administrator for the network. This is a very technical position that requires prerequisite knowledge of a network operating system, at least several months formal training, at least 6 months apprenticeship training with an experienced network manager, and a clearance procedure since the administrator will have access to highly sensitive corporate data. The network administrator must have access to everything on the network, including data, to practically administer the network and troubleshoot it during emergencies. This makes the network administrator a weak link in the security chain. The network administrator will have to be trained on each operating system, various software packages, and network monitoring equipment in order to use it effectively. Training the network or systems administrator using a guide for INFOSEC Best Practices will assure that all aspects of security are addressed in a consistent manner from one administrator to the next. The administrator must also be aware of day to day operational issues such as how backups are done and how the network is used.

✓ INFOSEC Best Practice #192

INFOSEC Best Practices must include emergency procedures that must be followed when information security is compromised.

When it is revealed that there is a hacker attack or information security is compromised, then the network security administrator must quickly know what to do. In order to have some guidance on what to do, emergency procedures must be compiled for reference. Emergency procedures must include procedures for spamming, operating system security breach, destruction or corruption of a network operating system, virus introduction, deletion of data, and password disclosure. Include the use of mock scenarios in your training sessions and see how well the systems staff responds.

INFOSEC Best Practice #193

Maintain a retraining schedule for system administrators.

One-time training for each system administrator may not be enough. System administrators must have periodic training on information security best practices. These best practices will change as technology changes and the retraining will keep everyone current.

 INFOSEC Best Practice #194

Review security training manuals and procedures regularly.

Security procedures and training manuals will need to be updated regularly as new vulnerabilities are discovered, new systems are released, or your site's security policy changes.

Emergency Rules Against Attacks

Emergency procedures or countermeasures must be used when a network or computer is compromised. These emergency procedures may seem drastic, but can save downtime and prevent the destruction of information.

✔ INFOSEC Best Practice #195

> If you suspect your site is being probed, then turn on logging and run intrusion detection software.

If you suspect that your site is being probed, then make sure that security logging is turned on. The intrusion detection software must notify you via your beeper of any suspicious activity so that you can react quickly to the situation. Investing in an intrusion detection software package may give you the warning you need before too much damage is done by the hacker(s).

✔ INFOSEC Best Practice #196

> If you are in the process of being spammed, stop your post office process on the mail server.

If you are being attacked by mail bombs or being spammed, then the mail server disk may be filling up and the CPU may be overloaded. By stopping the post-office process on the mail server, you will stop the server from accepting any new mail via port 25. It will give you time to try to protect the computer against the suspected attack and, in the event of spamming, clean up your hard disk by deleting the junk mail. Also, create a separate disk partition for all user email.

 INFOSEC Best Practice #197

> If you suspect that you are having illegal telnet sessions, then shut the telnet service off.

A telnet session requires users to log into a computer from a remote computer. If someone is using telnet to gain access to your computer, then the external user may have learned an account name and password to your system. Immediately change passwords to suspected accounts, especially system accounts.

 INFOSEC Best Practice #198

> If you suspect that there is an attack on your system through your open TCP/IP ports, then filter out access to these ports via a firewall or shut down services associated with those ports.

If a system is under attack via TCP/IP port access, then you should disconnect the system from the network and disable the services that are using those ports since they may have security holes. Also, tighten up access to those services through your firewall rules. Only allow access between known and authenticated sites.

✔ INFOSEC Best Practice #199

If you are suspecting that someone is illegally logging into many systems, then shut down access to your modem server and require password changes.

If someone is illegally logging into your network through your modems, then a password has been compromised. Temporarily disable remote logins, and then change the passwords for remote login users.

✔ INFOSEC Best Practice #200

If you experience a denial of service attack, then disconnect the computer from the network and perform an immediate analysis to determine if there is a quick way of filtering out the packets via your filtering router.

If you notice that your system is unresponsive due to a massive flood of packets to your system, then the first step is to disconnect your system from the network. The internet router logs should be analyzed to determine the source of the packets and those addresses should be filtered out.

These addresses are probably not the primary source of the attack, but hacked systems which are being used by the attacker. Stopping the attack for the immediate future will allow you to reconnect to the internet while you perform a more in-depth analysis. This does not guarantee that the attack will not resume through a different system, but buys you time to analyze the attack more thoroughly and put in rules at your router that can filter out similar patterns of attack. The attack should be reported to FIRST, CERT or, depending on the intensity and maliciousness of the attack, to the FBI National Infrastructure Protection Center (NIPC) (see Appendix A for contact information).

✔ INFOSEC Best Practice #201

> If the denial of service attack is uploading large files via FTP to fill the disk, then disable logins and either create a partition that uses only a portion of the disk for file transfer or set disk quotas for the user.

First disable logins, and then limit the disk space available for FTP downloads. This can be done by either setting disk quotas if your operating system supports this feature, or creating a disk partition that is used for FTP downloads. If this partition fills up, then no more data can be placed in that partition, but the operating system will be unaffected and the system will run. If this type of attack is done via a specific user login, then disable that account. If the user calls about not being able to gain access, then you can discuss the problem of a disk space limit or change the password of the account if it is suspected that the account is being used by an unauthorized user.

INFOSEC Best Practice #202

> If the denial of service attack is causing large error messages to be written in a log file that fills up the disk, then create a disk partition specifically for your log file(s).

If you are being attacked in a way that causes your system to write large error messages to a log file that eventually fills up the disk, then create a disk partition specifically for your log file(s) and designate the system to write data to those files in the new location. As the log files fill up the disk partition, the rest of the system is unaffected. These types of attacks may also cause your system to run slowly by using a large number of CPU cycles, or sometimes they may crash the machine. If this is the case, then disconnect the machine from the network, reboot, clean up the log files, and limit the size of the log files to a reasonable size. Limiting the size of a log file will prevent too many CPU cycles from being used. Finally, you may have to monitor the network to see what IP address is contacting your machine and causing this problem and filter that address out in your firewall. If the attack continues and comes from different IP addresses, then contact the authorities.

 INFOSEC Best Practice #203

> If the denial of service attack is consuming your network through a flood ping attack, then disconnect your internal network from the internet.

A flood ping attack will overwhelm your network with ping packets that can consume your network bandwidth and consume the destination computer's CPU cycles. Disconnect your network from the internal network. A temporary remedy can be to filter all packets that are being sent to the destination computer. If the IP source of the ping is known, then all packets from that source can be filtered. Once filtering at the firewall is set, then reconnect your network. If attacks continue from multiple or changing sources, then contact the authorities.

✓ **INFOSEC Best Practice #204**

> If the denial of service attack is locking up ports on your computer through a SYN flood attack, then disconnect your computer from the network and filter packets from the source address at the firewall.

If you suspect a SYN flood attack from the symptom of ports locking up, then disconnect your computer from the network. Analyze network packets to try to determine the source address of SYN packets destined for the computer with the symptom and filter those packets from the source via your firewall.

✓ **INFOSEC Best Practice #205**

> If various types of problems are affecting performance and reliability of your computer and they do not appear hardware related, then run the latest patches (i.e., service packs) for your operating system and internet-related software.

Some problems are difficult to diagnose and may be suspected as being hardware related. If you can't find any problem with your hardware and yet system reliability and performance are affected, then you may have hackers exploiting known software bugs to run malicious code. Update the system with the latest service packs for your operating system and internet-related software products.

ACRONYM LIST

ACL   Access Control List, grants access to file or object to anyone in list associated with a file or object.

COTS   Commercial Off The Shelf hardware or software

B1   Labeled Security Protection as specified in DoD 5200.28-STD

C2   Controlled Access Protection as specified in DoD 5200.28-STD

DES   Data Encryption Standard

DMS   Defense Messaging System

DMZ   De-Militarized Zone

FTP   File Transport Protocol

Guard   A computer that has a set of controls that mediate trusted transfers across security boundaries.

HTTP   Hypertext Transfer Protocol

S-HTTP   Secure Hypertext Transfer Protocol

INFOSEC Information Security

Kerberos A secret key based service for providing authentication in a network

MLS   MultiLevel Security pertaining to classification levels

NES	Network Encryption System, a hardware encryption device by Motorola approved for encryption of Secret data over public networks
NFS	Network File System, a utility that permits files on a remote system to be accessed as though they were local
NNTP	Network News Transport Protocol
PEM	Privacy enhanced Mail, adds encryption, source authentication, and integrity protection to mail text messages.
Perimeter Subnet	Isolated network segment between two screening routers where public accessible computers can be placed
PGP	Pretty Good Privacy, secure mail protocol
POP3	Post Office Protocol for transferring mail between server and client
RAS	Remote Access Service in Windows NT
RPC	Remote Procedure Call
SBU	Sensitive But Unclassified
Screening Router	Performs packet filtering according to a set of rules set by the administrator
SMB	Server Message Block, NT net protocol for passing info on computers
SMTP	Simple Mail Transport Protocol, used to transfer mail between servers

SSL   Secure Sockets Layer

Telnet   A protocol for acting as a terminal on a remote system

TCP/IP   Transport Control Protocol/Internet Protocol

WWW   World Wide Web

BIBLIOGRAPHY

Abene, Mark, Kovacich, G. L. and Lutz, S. "Intrusion Detection Provides a Pound of Prevention," *Network Computing Online: The Technology Solutions Center.* 1997.

Alexander, Michael. *The Underground Guide to Computer Security.* Addison-Wesley Publishing Company, 1996.

Allen, Julia, *The CERT® Guide to System and Network Security Practices*, Addison-Wesley, 2001.

Amoroso, Edward G. *Intrusion Detection: An Introduction to Internet Surveillance, Correlation, Traps, Trace Back, and Response.* Intrusion.net Books, 1999.

Anonymous, *Maximum Linux Security: A Hacker's Guide to Protecting Your Linux Server and Workstation.* Sams, 1999.

Bellovin, Steve. "Security Problems in the TCP/IP Protocol Suite," *Computer Communication Review.* Vol. 19, No. 2, April 1989.

Bhimani, Anish B., Schultz, E. and Siegal, C. *Internet Security for Business.* Ed.: Terry Bernstein. John Wiley & Sons, 1996.

Chapman, D. B. and Zwicky, E. D. *Building Internet Firewalls.* O'Reilly & Associates, Inc., 1995.

Cooper, F., Goggans, C., Halvey. J. K., Hughes, L., Morgan, L., Siyan, K., Stallings, W., Stephenson, P. *Implementing Internet Security.* New Riders Publishing, 1995.

Curry, David. *UNIX System Security.* Addison Wesley, 1992.

Denning, Dorothy E. *Information Warfare and Security.* Addison-Wesley Publishing Company, 1998.

Department of Defense (DoD). *Department of Defense Trusted Computer System Evaluation Criteria.* DoD 5200.28-STD, 1985.

Department of Defense (DoD). *Department of Defense Password Management Guideline.* CSC-STD-002-85, 1985.

Department of Defense (DoD). *Computer Security Requirements: Guidance for Applying the Department of Defense Trusted Computer System Evaluation Criteria in Specific Environments.* CSC-STD-003-85, 1985.

Department of Defense (DoD). Technical Rational Behind CSC-STD-003-85: *Computer Security Requirements. Guidance for Applying the Department of Defense Trusted Computer System Evaluation Criteria in Specific Environments.* CSC-STD-004-85, 1985.

Department of Defense (DoD). *National Industrial Security Program Operating Manual (NISPOM), 1993.*

Department of Defense (DoD). 1993. *Green Book Draft 4.0.* Office of the Vice President of the United States, Federal Internet Security: A Framework for Action. Draft, 1995.

Defense Information Systems Agency (DISA). Technical Memorandum. *Security Guard Survey.* August 1995.

Escamilla, Terry. *Intrusion Detection: Network Security Beyond the Firewall.* John Wiley and Sons, 1998.

Garfinkel, Simson and Spafford, G. *Practical UNIX and Internet Security.* O'Reilly & Associates, Inc., 1996.

Garfinkel, Simson and Spafford, G. *Web Security and Commerce.* O'Reilly and Associates, Inc., 1997.

Gurley Bace, Rebecca. *Intrusion Detection.* Macmillan Technical Publishing, 1999.

Hughes, Larry J. *Actually Useful Internet Security Techniques.* New Riders Publishing, 1995.

Kaufman, C., Perlman, R. and Speciner, M. *Network Security: Private Communication in a Public World.* Prentice Hall, 1995.

Kabay, Michel E. *The NCSA Guide to Enterprise Security: Protecting Information Assets.* McGraw Hill, 1996.

McClure, Stuart, Scambray, J. and Kurtz, G. *Hacking Exposed: Network Security Secrets and Solutions.* McGraw-Hill, 1999.

Meinel, C., *"How Hackers Break In..."*, Scientific American, October 1998, pp. 98-105.

Northcutt, Stephen and S. Northcult. *Network Intrusion Detection: An Analysis Handbook.* New Riders Publishing, 1999.

Peltier, Thomas R., *Information Security Policies, Procedures, and Standards*, CRC Press, 2001.

Sutton S., Trusted Systems Services, Inc., *Windows NT Security Guide,* Addison-Wesley Developers Press, 1997.

APPENDIX A

This appendix contains a number of useful urls related to information security.

Incidence Response Centers

CERT Coordination Center
http://www.cert.org
cert@cert.org

Computer Incident Advisory Capability (CIAC)
http://ciac.llnl.gov/
ciac@llnl.gov

Defense Information Systems Agency
Center for Automated System Security
http://www.assist/mil
cert@cert.mil

FBI – National Infrastructure Protection Center (NIPC)
http://www.fbi.gov/nipc/
nipc@fbi.gov

Federal Computer Incidence Response Center
http://www.fedcirc.gov/
fedcirc@fedcirc.gov

Forum of Incidence Response and Security Teams (FIRST)
http://www.first.org/
first-sec@first.org

Vulnerability Sites

http://www.iss.net/cgi-bin/xforce
http://cve.mitre.org
http://www.cs.purdue.edu/coast/projects/vdb.html
http://seclab.cs.ucdavis.edu/projects/vulnerabilities/#database/

Security Sites

http://www.sans.org
http://www.securityportal.com
http://www.nsi.org/compsec.html
http://www.cerias.purdue.edu/coast
http://www.icsa.net
http://cs-www.ncsa.nist.gov/

Hacker Sites

These sites may lead you to tools and techniques hackers use to break into sites. You may want to use these tools to test your system and network security.

http://www.hackers.com	(Hackers.com)
http://www.cultdeadcow.com	(Cult of the Dead Cow)
http://www.defcon.org	(Def Con)
http://www.10pht.com	(LOPHT Heavy Industries)
http://www.2600.com	(2600 magazine)
http://www.phrack.com	(Phrack Magazine)
http://www.hackernews.com	(Hacker News Network)

Mailing Lists

CERT Advisories: cert-advisory-request@cert.org
CIAC Advisories: majordomo@rumpole.llnl.gov
COAST Security Archive: coast-request@cs.purdue.edu
FreeBSD Security Issues: majordomo@freebsd.org

APPENDIX B
Sample Security Policy

Purpose

The purpose of establishing this information security policy for *CORPORATION X* is to protect corporate information and computer assets while allowing: 1) e-mail communication, 2) information transfer, and 3) access to the corporate website and web-based e-commerce server between customers, corporate affiliates, and corporate users. Also, it defines policies for protecting data within the corporation and addresses the confidentiality, data integrity, availability, accountability, and responsibility issues that each employee must be aware of and comply with while working for this corporation.

Threats

1. Virus introduced by e-mail, web browsing, corporate web-site access, floppy, CD, tape, or ftp downloads.

2. Denial of service attacks from the internet to corporate servers.

3. Unauthorized login into computers by learned or hacked usernames and passwords for the purpose of reading, deleting, removing, or inserting data not approved by the responsible party of the computer resource.

4. Unauthorized network access to server and workstation computers for the purpose of reading, deleting, removing, or inserting data not approved by the responsible party of the computer resource.

5. Unauthorized physical access to corporate servers that may result in inadvertent or malicious shutoff, damage, or login access to the server.

6. Unauthorized access to data by a user because of lack of file protection.

7. Loss of data assurance (i.e., receipt of data without traceability) of confidential corporate data during network transfer.

8. Loss of data integrity (i.e., data tampered with during transmission) of confidential corporate data during network transfer.

9. Theft of disks and tapes.

10. Unauthorized tampering with network resources that can lead to the loss of the network.

11. Loss of power.

12. Lightning strike.

13. Illness of personnel that may lead to users bypassing information security for the sake of convenience.

Cost/Benefit Analysis

The calculated cost of the e-commerce server being down every minute is $_____.

The calculated cost of the network being down every minute is $_____.

The calculated cost of removing a virus from a single PC is $_____. The cost for removing a virus from all corporate machines is $_____.

The calculated cost of e-mail being down per user per day is $_____.

The calculated cost of secret corporate information getting into the hands of a competitor is $_____.

These are considered the primary risks due to financial loss for the following information security measures.

Confidentiality

1. Corporate servers must be located in a secure physical location with access only by authorized personnel via combination lock or access card.

2. A firewall must separate corporate computers and servers from the internet.

3. All users must have a separate user account and password that must be kept confidential.

4. Each server must have an account policy that enforces passwords to be a minimum of 6 alphanumeric characters long.

5. Each server must have an account policy that enforces password expiration every 3 months.

6. Each server must keep a password history file that saves the history of a user's passwords and does not allow reuse.

7. Users cannot share accounts.

8. All user accounts will use password-protected screen savers.

9. Users may not access another user's data without permission. Each server must have a file protection system that restricts user access to the user's own files. Exceptions include a user belonging to a group that has file access via group file permissions.

10. Users must take responsibility to protect their data.

11. All corporate confidential data must be encrypted with 128-bit encryption before being transmitted over a public communication channel (e.g., the internet, leased lines, or POTS connections).

12. All corporate confidential email must use PGP encryption. Public keys must be posted to the PKI system at the following server ldap://certserver.pgp.com. Day to day email does not have to be encrypted.

13. Financial servers and servers with highly classified corporate information must reside on a separate network that is physically separate from any corporate network that is connected to the internet.

14. No e-mail or internet access is allowed on corporate financial servers and servers with highly classified corporate information.

15. Workstations and servers behind the corporate firewall must not have a modem connection. Modem connections will be handled via an authorized dial-in server.

Integrity

1. The administrator and alternate administrator account must be the only accounts with access to all files.

2. All file transfers of highly confidential data between machines must check for the integrity of the data.

3. System files must be read-execute for users.

4. Any new data copied onto a server must be done through the server that must log the transaction.

5. All systems must have anti-virus software present that scans all disks, floppy drives, incoming IP traffic, and MS Word macros.

6. Confidential data must be encrypted during data transfer.

7. No unapproved software shall be installed on any workstation without authorization from the corporate MIS department.

Availability

1. Dial-in capability will be to a specified dial-in server that will authenticate the user.

2. Each server must have an uninterruptible power supply (UPS).

3. All servers must be available 24 x 7 x 365.

4. Access to e-mail, FTP, and HTTP services must be available 24 hours per day.

5. Each server must be in a room with controlled access.

6. The servers and workstations in the internal network must have proxy services for designated users coming in outside the firewall. Database servers may be accessed by specific IP addresses that are authorized to access the resources using FTP or HTTP. These addresses must use gateway authentication at the firewall in order to gain access to servers inside the firewall.

7. Access to servers on the internal network must be restricted by a firewall that specifies the IP address that may pass and requires authentication.

8. If IT personnel are not available during an emergency, then there will be a backup person(s) that will be assigned to the task.

Accountability

1. All account security events must be logged.

2. All confidential file access must be logged.

3. All data transfers of confidential data must use authentication between server and client.

4. All confidential data sent to another machine must have a digital signature associated with it.

5. All new software deployed on either servers or workstations must be authorized by the IT staff. A software log of installed software must be maintained.

6. All connections through the firewall must be logged.

Recovery

1. All server data will be backed up daily using incremental back-ups.

2. Full backups will be done once a week.

3. Archives will be done monthly.

4. Backups and archives must be stored off-site.

5. Desktop workstations will use network file services to store corporate data that should be backed up by the server.

6. Desktop workstations will have standardized configurations for each department that will include designated versions of the operating system at a specified revision level, anti-virus software, e-mail and groupware software, word processing and spreadsheet software, and other specific departmental software. An image of this software configuration will be made by MIS. This image will be pushed down to the departmental workstation in the event of operating system corruption.

Employee Responsibilities

1. Employees must adhere to the stated policy as technology changes and must make best efforts to protect data and not indulge in activities that compromise data.

2. Employees should backup any data that they feel is important that is not stored on the corporate file servers.

3. Employees must comply with the corporate information security policy.

4. Copyrighted software must be used in accordance with the software license.

5. Corporate computers cannot be used for personal purposes.

6. Corporate e-mail cannot be used for personal purposes.

7. The hardware configuration of a desktop workstation cannot be changed without approval from the MIS department.

8. Employees are prohibited from transmitting fraudulent, obscene or harassing messages to anyone.

9. Employees are prohibited from transmitting programs to anyone that have the intent of compromising information security or disrupting work.

Enforcement

1. Any reported abuses of corporate resources will be investigated. During the investigation the company may access the electronic file of its employee. If computer policy has been violated then the employee's privileges may be restricted as decided by the CIO.

2. The company will audit resources periodically to ensure that software and computer configurations comply with policy.

Education

1. Information security training will be provided by the company once a year.

2. Each employee will receive a hard copy of the corporate information security policy and must read it.

Configuration Issues

1. The corporate internal network will contain networked workstations that need to access the internet, and servers running
   databases, file, printer services, administrative purchase order
   submittal system, and expense reporting system.

2. The corporate network will have a firewall between the corporate network and internet connection.

3. Publicly accessible servers such as the web server, e-commerce
   server, e-mail server, and FTP server must be located on a DMZ
   within the firewall.

4. Mail applications must support PGP encryption as an option.

5. All computers will have anti-virus software installed.

6. Data communication between machines with confidential data
   must be encrypted using 128-bit encryption.

7. Network printer cards must have their default access password
   changed.

8. All network devices must be SNMP compliant.

Glossary

Access Control - Operating systems limit access to computer system resources and services by authentication of the user and other access rules.

ACL - Access Control List, grants access to file or object to anyone in list associated with a file or object.

ACK - Acknowledgment. A packet of information sent from a receiving computer that acknowledges receipt of data.

Anonymous Remailer - A program that removes an email message's sender and location before sending the message to the destination.

Application Gateway - A program that restricts access to services across a firewall boundary.

Authentication - The process of verifying the identity of a user before access is allowed to a system.

Authorization - After authentication, the user is allowed the use of specific system resources that have been granted to that user.

Backdoor - Once a hacker breaks into a system, code can be inserted somewhere on the system to create a secret backdoor that allows unauthorized access.

Bastion Host - A computer usually located on the DMZ that often hosts the web site, email or a gateway to the network that has very high security features. It is often a machine that is accessed by the public or is the first line of defense to your network.

Confidentiality - Assurance of privacy of information (usually by encryption).

COTS - Commercial Off The Shelf hardware or software.

B1 - Labeled Security Protection as specified in DoD 5200.28-STD

Certificate Authority - A trusted system that digitally signs certificates to validate ownership of a public key.

C2 - Controlled Access Protection as specified in DoD 5200.28-STD.

Cookie - A confidential password or key.

DES - Data Encryption Standard.

Digital Signature - An electronic signature that authenticates a sender of a message and ensures integrity of the message.

DNS - Domain Name System. System to map IP addresses to host names.

DMS - Defense Messaging System.

DMZ - De-Militarized Zone.

Denial of Service Attacks - Denial of service attacks disable a computer system by eating system resources until the system or applications come to a halt.

Dual-homed Gateway - A computer with two network interfaces each of which is connected to a separate network that provides a point at which data can be filtered or blocked between the two networks.

Encryption - The process of converting data from plain text (readable data) to coded text (ciphertext) by using a cipher (encryption algorithm). The ciphertext can only be read by decrypting it.

Decryption - The process of converting ciphertext to plain text usually by use of a key.

File Server - A networked computer that is the central data depository for files or data that is used by networked computers on a network.

Firewall - A system of computers that protects an internal trusted network from an external untrusted network by blocking and filtering traffic from the untrusted network.

FTP - File Transport Protocol.

Gateway - A computer that passes data between networks. A router is considered a gateway.

Guard - A computer that has a set of controls that mediate trusted transfers across security boundaries.

Hacker - A person that attempts to attack a target system by breaching its security with intent to cause damage or disruption of service.

Host - A computer connected to a network.

HTTP - Hypertext Transfer Protocol.

S-HTTP - Secure Hypertext Transfer Protocol.

INFOSEC - Information Security.

IP Address - a 32-bit address that uniquely identifies a host on an IP network.

Data Integrity - A comparison of data to its original state.

Kerberos - A secret key based service for providing authentication in a network.

Key - A password that is used by an encryption algorithm to determine how plain text is encrypted or ciphertext decrypted.

MLS - MultiLevel Security pertaining to classification levels.

Name Resolution - The process of mapping a host name to an IP address (DNS is used by the Internet to do name resolution).

NES - Network Encryption System, a hardware encryption device by Motorola approved for encryption of Secret data over public networks.

NFS - Network File System, a utility that permits files on a remote system to be accessed as though they were local.

NNTP - Network News Transport Protocol.

Packet - A unit of data that is sent over a network.

Packet Sniffer - Sniffers are programs that monitor network traffic (i.e., packets) and can gather useful information that can be used in an attack.

PEM - Privacy enhanced Mail, adds encryption, source authentication, and integrity protection to mail text messages.

Perimeter Subnet - Isolated network segment between two screening routers where public accessible computers can be placed.

PGP - Pretty Good Privacy, secure mail protocol.

PKI - Public Key Infrastructure. An encryption system that consists of a keypair of a private key for encrypting data and a public key for decrypting data. Public keys can be maintained privately by a corporation or on public servers accessible on the internet.

Plain Text - Text that is readable to the user.

POP3 - Post Office Protocol for transferring mail between server and client.

Port - A TCP/IP transport layer value (port number) that is a unique number associated with an application running on a computer (e.g., HTTP = 80).

Protocol - A set of rules that specify how computers will communicate over a network.

Protocol Stack - A layered set of protocols that work together to enable applications to communicate over the network.

Proxy - A software program that typically resides on a computer between the user and the destination computer and establishes a connection to the destination computer on behalf of a user while applying a set of rules to determine whether the user is permitted connection for a specific type of service (e.g., http, SMTP, POP, etc).

RAS - Remote Access Service in Windows NT.

Router - A piece of network hardware that delivers packets between a sending and receiving computer. These computers are on separate network and the router is used to determine how to "route" the destination packet to the appropriate network on which the receiving computer resides.

RPC - Remote Procedure Call.

SBU - Sensitive But Unclassified.

Screening Router - Performs packet filtering according to a set of rules set by the administrator.

SMB - Server Message Block, NT net protocol for passing info on computers

SMTP - Simple Mail Transport Protocol, used to transfer mail between servers.

Spoofing - This is a form of attack that involves the subtle alteration of data in a packet. A sophisticated hacker may be able to alter the data effectively in order to do damage to the intended target.

Socket - A bi-directional communication mechanism for data used by TCP/IP that enables multiple applications to access the network at the same time.

SSL - Secure Sockets Layer.

Subnet - A network segment that shares a network address with other portions of the network.

Sweeper - Hackers may use a program called a *sweeper* that sweeps (i.e., deletes) all data from the system.

Telnet - A protocol for acting as a terminal on a remote system.

TCP/IP - Transport Control Protocol/Internet Protocol.

Trojan Horse - Trojan horses are software codes that enter the computer system through the front door via a program or utility that the user believes to be harmless such as a text editor or useful utility program. When the program is used, it then performs some malicious function such as deleting or copying files to another computer.

Tunneling - A system that routes traffic by encrypting it for transmission across an untrusted network such as the internet and then decrypts it at the receiving end.

Virus - Computer viruses are compact packages of software that require a host (i.e., the computer) in order to replicate and possibly cause damage.

WAN - Wide Area Network. A network that usually spans large geographic areas.

Worm - Once inside a computer a hacker can place a program called a *worm* that self-replicates. Worm programs keep growing larger until disk space or memory is filled.

WWW - World Wide Web.

Index

E

email bombing, 1
emergency procedures, 153
enforcement, 15
Ethernet, 48
EXE, 2

F

FAT, 2
FBI National Infrastructure Protection
    Center (NIP, 156
FILE, 25
filtering firewall, 32
filtering router, 20
filtering rules, 20
financial data, 34
financial loss, 11
fire protection systems, 45
firewall, 8
FIRST, 156
FTP, 25, 29
ftp, 4
FTP server, 108
FTP serving, 28

G

gateway, 25

H

HTTP, 29
hubs, 39

I

integrity, 15
internal network, 24
InterNIC, 7
Intranet mail, 28
intrusion detection software, 153
IP, 4
IP address ranges, 91

IP packets, 20
IP spoofing, 4
IPX, 57

J

Java applets, 114

K

Kerberos, 75

L

LAN, 35
"likelihood" matrix, 14

M

macros, 2
mail encryption software, 104
mail server, 102
Mail servers, 28
Maintenance, 141
MD4, 62
MIS, 34
mission-critical, 17
mission-critical custom software, 119
mission-critical machines, 9
modem communication protocol, 62
modem security, 60
modem server, 36
Modem telephone numbers, 60
modems, 9

N

NCSA, 30
NetBios, 57
network backbone wiring, 47
network devices, 50
network file access permissions, 83
network file systems, 89
Network monitoring, 137
network printers, 59
networks, 9

new wiring, 47
NEWS, 25, 115
NFS, 26, 90
NNTP, 115
non-promiscuous network interfaces, 59

P

packet-screening routers, 20
Password cracking programs, 8
password expiration, 72
password history, 73
password length, 74
passwords, 3
personal data, 51
physical security, 43
PIN/Synchronous, 70
private key, 130, 131
proxy server, 30
public key, 130

R

RAS, 62
Remote Access Server, 62
remote administration, 82
risk analysis, 14
rlogin, 4
rsh, 26

S

S/Key, 70
screen saver, 80
screening router, 25
Screening routers, 56
security classifications, 129
Security hardware, 41
security logger, 93
security policy, 11, 13
security software, 41
sensitive information, 34
separate logical partitions, 22
server certificates, 130

shielded wiring, 49
SHTTP, 112
single network segment, 21
SMTP, 29
Sniffers, 4
SNMP, 57, 139
software-tracking programs, 133
Spamming, 1
spoofing, 4
SSL, 112
surge suppressors, 44
sweeper, 4
switch, 21
switches, 57
SYN, 4
system administrators, 81

T

tamper-resistant, 17
TCP ports, 32
TCP service port, 20
TCP/IP, 4, 57
telnet, 4, 25, 29
TELNET proxy server, 110
TELNET session, 33
"Tempest" shielding, 46
threat analysis, 14
top-secret information, 46
training, 149
transmission speed, 48
Trojan horses, 5
true floor, 45

U

uninterruptable power supplies, 44
UNIX, 56
usernames, 8

V

virtual file services, 90
virtual private networks, 29
virus databases, 88

virus scanner, 86
viruses, 2
VPN, 29
vulnerability analysis, 12

W

WAN, 35
websites, 28
whois, 7
Wide Area Network, 35
wireless, 49
worm, 3

X

X-Windows, 26, 91

Z

zone transfer, 8